RECLAIMING

THE CLASSROOM

How America's Teachers Lost Control of Education

and How They Can Get It Back

TRENTON GOBLE

with Timothy Robinson & Cindi Dunford

ISBN: 1519636687
ISBN-13: 978-1519636683

ABOUT
THE AUTHOR

TRENTON GOBLE, MASTERYCONNECT

co-founder and chief learning officer

Trenton spent 20 years in Utah as a teacher, principal, and district administrator. He and his team travel the country working with teachers and administrators to implement mastery learning and advocate for those who do the important work of educating our children.

ACKNOWLEDGMENT

I WANT TO EXPRESS MY DEEPEST GRATITUDE to everyone who has directly or indirectly influenced the message of this book. You have been my students, my colleagues, my mentors and my friends.

I am especially grateful to those at MasteryConnect who granted me the time and resources to make this dream a reality.

Most of all I want to thank Amy, Elliot, and Maggie.

FOREWORD

I RECEIVED A CALL YEARS AGO FROM A GENTLEMAN in the process of staffing leadership positions for a new school district in the area where my child would be attending school. He asked me a few general questions about a young and promising administrator by the name of Trenton Goble. I had worked with Trenton for years and knew him well, so when the man asked if I thought Trenton would be a good fit as the director of elementary education in the recently-created district, my response was, "If you are looking for a progressive, creative, brilliant mind that thinks outside of the box and challenges norms and traditions in ways that make people reflect on their beliefs and practices, then Trenton is certainly the kind of person you are looking for!"

Reclaiming the Classroom should strike a nerve with every educator concerned with the current state of education. Trenton draws from decades of experience as he vividly traces through history society's loss of trust in educators. But Trenton also gives us direction as to where we can go and why we should want to go there. "Students watch teachers every day. They see teachers at their best and at their worst. They act as teachers act. If students are to learn the skills they need to succeed not just in school, but in life in general, and if teachers are to successfully own their accountability and reclaim their classrooms, then teachers need a return to the ability to collaborate—not compete—with their colleagues, and they need respect from their peers and superiors. Teachers need the return of autonomy, mastery, and purpose."

Trenton's message resonates with teachers who see themselves as capable and caring professionals; teachers who recognize that the focus of the work we do in our schools should be true student learning, improved instruction, and meaningful relationships, *not* high-stakes testing. Trenton inspires teachers to step up and lead the charge to own their accountability and re-establish trust with their communities.

This book was written by an educator for educators in a way that enlightens, inspires, and motivates all of us who genuinely love what we do, and who we do it for, to reclaim our classrooms. It is a call to action to *finally* do the right thing, for ourselves and most important, for our children.

STEVE GILES
Principal, Blackridge Elementary School

TABLE OF CONTENTS

INTRODUCTION

TEACHING IS AN INTIMATE ACT AND REQUIRES A CONNECTION BETWEEN TWO PEOPLE. The people involved are a teacher and a student. Not an administrator. Not a legislator. Not a secretary of education. Not the president of anything.

There is one person: a student, who may or may not have any interest in actually learning anything. And there is another person: a teacher, whose job it is to get through and not only inspire that student to *want* to learn, but to figure out *how* that particular student learns and use that method, whatever it turns out to be, to help her learn what she needs to know.

There may be a room full of students around that one student. There may be, if some reformers have their way, literally hundreds of students around that student, all vying for the attention of the same teacher. But that doesn't change the nature of teaching. There is still only one student and one teacher—just iterated a couple hundred times.

How does the teacher do this? How does the teacher find out how each individual student needs to learn? Through intuition and experimentation. That is the work of teaching.

This book is titled *Reclaiming the Classroom* because other forces have been reaching into America's classrooms to dictate the terms of the relationship between the teacher and the student. Testing regimes and federal mandates have replaced teacher syllabi. An exclusive focus on math and language arts (the tested subjects) is eclipsing attention to science, social studies, history, music, and art. Formulaic growth calculations have taken the place of direct accountability to parents and school boards. The role of teachers has been demeaned and diminished.

Teachers are threatened by attitudes that hold them as self-interested government workers. They are threatened by reform administrations that view them as a big part of the problem rather than the solution. They are threatened by the promise that new technologies can make their work obsolete. The whole discussion about the quality of American education that is taking place in capitol chambers and boardrooms and campaign headquarters around the country is largely taking place without teacher input.

But the time has come for teachers—those women and men actually in the arena—to reclaim the classroom.

You could say that this is a book about the soul of America. You could say that America's soul is in our classrooms every school day where the terms of our republic are put to the test—things like liberty, equality, economic opportunity—to see if we really mean what we said in the Constitution. You could say that the promise of America has to be ratified, not by any constitutional convention, or even by the states, but by America's children who are seeking to find their way. You could say that teachers are the ones who make our republic, the ones who enforce its values— values taught, to be sure, by most of the parents in the home, but needing to be worked out in the public sphere, not of commerce (not yet) but of school. You could say that.

But it would still just be teachers and students in a classroom.

A SERIES OF COMPLEX HUMAN EVENTS

Anyone who heard the late Don DeLay speak heard him say a thousand times, "Teaching is a series of complex human events." This is true. But teaching also boils down at its most fundamental level to three actions:

① Identify student levels of understanding

② Target students for intervention

③ Evaluate teacher practice

On the surface, these are pretty straightforward and support what we're currently doing in schools, ensuring that all students are college and career ready. They condense teaching into a perfect thirty-second sound bite of what teachers do.

But if we go below the surface, what do these statements really *mean*? DeLay envisioned teaching as "an art form in understanding and responding to student engagement and the learning process in the social context of a classroom" (Donald DeLay obituary, 2011). Teachers welcome students from all walks of life—from all socioeconomic backgrounds, from all races and cultures, from all levels of intellect and intrinsic motivation. And these students all enter one teacher's classroom, creating a unique environment that is never again repeated. These unique combinations create the "series of complex human events" DeLay referred to. So how do these three actions address this deeper understanding of teaching?

Identify student levels of understanding. Students enter a classroom with varying levels of aptitude and attitude about any given subject. Identifying student levels of understanding goes beyond just identifying if a student can do long division. It reaches into whether a student has given consent to teach him long division, whether he's emotionally and intellectually ready to learn.

Target students for intervention. What do you think of when you read this phrase? Remediation? Resource? Action? Do you think of this phrase in a positive or negative way? Targeting students for intervention goes beyond the often-applied connotations of the words *target* and *intervention*. *All* students can be targeted, from the most "remedial" to the most "advanced." All *domains* can be targeted, from the academic domain you probably thought of when you first read the statement to behavioral and motivational and social domains. Intervention is as much (or more) about a teacher's changed perception of how to teach as about a student's changed perception of how to learn. This leads to the final statement.

Evaluate teacher practice. Everyone's trying to figure out how to evaluate teacher practice. Value-added and growth models are some of the latest favorites. Brian Gill, Julie Bruch, and Kevin Booker (2013), of Mathematica Policy Research, readily admit that teacher effectiveness is a moving target when they indicate that "absent a true measure of teacher effectiveness, [our] literature review includes evidence on how closely alternative growth measures correlate with other measures of teacher effectiveness." But evaluating teacher practice isn't about *others* evaluating teacher practice, it's about *teachers* evaluating their *own* practice. About how we use data to inform our instruction. As teachers, we sometimes seem to forget that we are evaluators of our own practice as well as of our students' learning. In fact, we are in the best position to evaluate the "series of complex human events" that present themselves daily in our classrooms.

THE BIG THREE

With these broader understandings in mind, I introduce the foundation of this book, the **Big Three**:

- Identify student levels of *readiness* and understanding.

- Target students for *any needed* intervention.

- *Self*-evaluate *instructional* practice.

These Big Three aren't numbered. That's intentional. They're not a list. They don't have to go in any particular order. I may evaluate my instruction *before* targeting my students for intervention, for example. And teachers touch on them many times throughout the year—sometimes many times throughout one lesson!

The Big Three aren't new, either. They're grounded in the elements of mastery-based learning. The Big Three simplify a very complex process into a nice, tidy talking point, with educators filling in the more complex blanks.

But teaching is under fire partly because the forces reaching into our classrooms don't fill in the blanks. They are only scratching at the surface of what it means to teach. These forces focus on only one domain—academic—and on only two subsets of this domain: math and English language arts. (Efforts are being made to expand this focus beyond math and English language arts, and to a lesser extent science, but these efforts are still only focusing on the academic domain.) This narrow focus fails to account for developmental and social and emotional and motivational reasons behind how a student learns. These forces are sending conflicting messages even within this narrow focus, emphasizing the need for personalized learning while steamrolling over teachers' abilities to provide just that by mandating standardized tests that force all students to be at the same place at the same time. These forces are tying teachers' hands by tying the results of this narrow focus to teachers' evaluations, forcing them at times to choose between teaching that meets students' needs and teaching that meets the requirements of external, high-stakes accountability.

The Big Three offer a solution to this misplaced focus and these conflicting messages. The Big Three represent solid, professional teaching that has always existed. Good teachers have always identified student levels of understanding, targeted students for intervention, and self-evaluated their instructional practice. But traditionally, they have shut their doors to do so. The solution to our current problems in education lies with teachers' implementation of the Big Three, but also with teachers' willingness to throw their doors open and visibly, publically lay claim to the accountability that is rightfully theirs.

Teachers once had the autonomy to meet the needs of individual students. But powerful and influential parts of our society have stepped in the way, thinking they're fixing what wasn't really broken in the first place. Reclaiming the Classroom traces society's journey from this initial place of trust to the external, high-stakes accountability we have today. I trace this journey from a personal perspective as well as from a historical one, explore some ideas about how we can find balance, and offer you a road back to autonomy and respect—a road you can take to reclaim your classroom. This journey is not a silver bullet because there is no silver bullet. There can be no simple, one-size-fits-all solution to a "series of complex human events." But there is a solution. It draws on The Big Three. And you are the key to reaching it. We'll get to this soon enough, but first, a little history.

CHAPTER 1

LOSING THE PUBLIC TRUST

THE SUMMER OF 1994. I remember it like it was yesterday. The heat from the June sun was baking the small, un-air-conditioned school from the outside in. The front doors and windows were wide open, and all the lights inside were off. As I exited my truck, I was greeted by the smell of warm asphalt mixed with a tinge of freshly cut grass. The musical chirping of sprinklers scattered across the playground. I could hear the melodic wind-chime sounds that you only get in the summer months when the tetherballs have been removed and the chains jingle against the poles as the wind blows past.

I instantly felt the sensation of belonging as I headed for the front doors. The aroma of floor wax, industrial cleaners, a hint of ditto fluid, and the residual smells of 600 children immediately consumed me. All of the lights were off in the building, but the reflection of light coming from the doorway at the end of the long, main hallway caused the newly waxed floors to look like a straight lazy brown river. Standing in the foyer of the school symbolized an end to years of preparation and the beginning of a career that would change everything I thought I knew about the teaching profession.

A quick stop in the front office allowed me to introduce myself to the school's head secretary, Mrs. Bills, who seemed to be sizing me up. Perhaps she wanted to know if the new guy was going to be able to cut it, or maybe she was just gathering information to share with the parents who were surely going to call and want the inside scoop on their child's sixth-grade teacher. After a few moments of small talk, Mrs. Bills handed me the keys to room 13 and pointed me in the right direction. Before heading to my classroom, I peeked into the gym/cafeteria and smiled as I began to imagine using the stage for plays and the gym for the physical education activities. After a short walk down the hall, I was standing in front of the door to my classroom. My classroom. It all seemed very surreal.

The classroom looked exactly like I had imagined: a large chalkboard in front with bulletin boards on either side. The far wall had a large bulletin board with windows on each side and built-in bookshelves running the entire length of the wall. The back wall had a sink with storage cabinets and a small bulletin board flanked by another large chalkboard. The near wall had two long rows of coat hangers and a large storage closet on each side of the doorway. The room was nearly empty except for a nearly new Apple LCII computer on the back counter and a teacher's desk in the front. The sweltering heat did little to dim my enthusiasm as it began to sink in—this was *my* classroom.

Like many new teachers, I thought I was ready. I had studied, written lesson plans, and spent countless hours in classrooms throughout my practicum and student teaching experiences. Any doubt about my readiness to teach was somehow lost in my youthful enthusiasm and belief that I was destined to change the world.

I don't recall much of my first year. I remember students and moments, but most of that first year is a blur. It wasn't a disaster or an unqualified success. I did OK, and I survived. Most important, I learned—a lot.

I learned that classroom management is critical. I wasn't organized, and my classroom lacked the simple routines that keep things running smoothly. I was constantly trying new things, and as a result, my students were always unsure of my expectations. That first year, I fell into a common trap: I worried about being liked. This often led me to second-guess my decisions to demand more from students when I thought they were slacking. I struggled to properly manage misbehavior. I struggled with consistency, I struggled with organization, I struggled to be prepared, and I pretty much struggled to survive.

I learned that teaching is hard, really hard. I gained a tremendous respect for the countless teachers I had observed throughout my life. I realized that many of the teachers I had thought were mediocre were dramatically better than I was. I also realized that great teachers are exceptionally skilled professionals. When you watch great teachers do what they do, you ultimately conclude that teaching is easy. They make everything look so damn simple.

I learned to be humble. I knew I had a long way to go, and I frankly wasn't prepared to suffer through another year of mediocrity. Throughout my first year, I kept a list of things I would never do again. It was long. I spent most of summer between my first and second years reflecting on all that I had learned and greeted my second year with eyes wide open. I was far more willing to ask for and listen to the advice of my peers.

I learned that becoming a good teacher is a process. Every day, we are given opportunities to try things that may or may not work, and over time, we become more attuned to what actually works. We begin to appreciate the unique needs of each individual student and learn to adjust our approach to meet those needs. Each new experience and challenge we face prepares us to become better teachers in the future. Eventually we realize that becoming a good teacher has less to do with how well we teach and more to do with how well we continue to learn.

THE LOSS OF AUTONOMY

I imagine most teachers have probably had a very similar experience. But I have watched over the years as this first-year ritual has slowly and subtly changed. During my first year, I had many positive interactions with my principal and district leadership. They were supportive and highly interested in my progress. I was fortunate to work with great colleagues who willingly provided resources, ideas, and constant encouragement. It was a safe place built on unquestioned trust and respect for those who accept the responsibilities that come with the keys to the classroom.

I have watched teachers slowly lose the trust and autonomy I enjoyed when I entered the profession in 1994. The education system has become paternalistic. Teachers are told what to teach and when to teach it, and are given strict timelines for completion in preparation for centrally aligned and created assessments. Data is crunched externally and presented in easily consumed charts and graphs. Many new teachers now enter the profession never having to create anything—it's all done for them. Some may see this as progress; it is not. Becoming a highly skilled teacher is a process. We learn as we create and try new things. To deny teachers this responsibility is to limit opportunities for growth. Efforts to centralize the most critical aspects of what it means to be a teacher has led to the McDonaldization of our classrooms—it isn't great, but at least it's the same.

No Child Left Behind ushered in the era of test-based accountability. The metrics for measuring quality teachers, schools, and districts relied on just one thing: improving test scores. It was a slippery slope. From the isolated confines of administrative offices and conference rooms, well-intentioned leaders began the process of slowly stripping teachers of one of their most fundamental responsibilities: mapping the curriculum. The risk that teachers may not focus on the right (tested) material was too great. School and district leaders began to hedge their bets, hoping that implementing greater control over what gets taught would improve test results. In doing so, they have been sending a very clear message to teachers: *We don't trust you.*

A NATIONAL RESOURCE

This wasn't always the case. Teachers weren't always mistrusted. There was a time when we viewed teachers as a great national resource. Over the course of almost 250 years of history, American public school teachers have been asked to do a lot of heavy lifting for the benefit of our nation. There's no mention of education in the Declaration of Independence, the Bill of Rights, or the Constitution—education has always been a matter for the states, according to the Tenth Amendment—but even though there's no mention of education in our founding documents, our founding *fathers* felt it was important for the safekeeping of our liberty and freedom. Thomas Jefferson advocated in Virginia for state-supported education in his 1779 *A Bill for the More General Diffusion of Knowledge:*

> The most effectual means of preventing [tyranny] would be, to illuminate, as far as practicable, the minds of the people at large... whence it becomes expedient for promoting the publick happiness that those persons, whom nature hath endowed with genius and

virtue, should be rendered by liberal education worthy to receive, and able to guard the sacred deposit of the rights and liberties of their fellow citizens, and that they should be called to that charge without regard to wealth, birth or other accidental condition or circumstance...it is better that such should be sought for and educated at the common expense of all, than that the happiness of all should be confined to the weak or wicked. (Honeywell, 1931) Jefferson's plan included free education for boys *and* girls for three years, with additional schooling available to students "at their private expense, as their parents, guardians, or friends shall think proper" (Honeywell, 1931). His bill also provided limited scholarships for students whose parents couldn't afford the additional schooling (Honeywell, 1931). Although the bill didn't pass at the time, its message about public education's role—teachers' roles—in safekeeping our liberty is clear.

Jefferson wasn't the only founding father to view education as a valuable resource. Forty years later, in a letter written to the Kentucky legislature, James Madison applauded Kentucky's efforts to provide public education for its children. In his letter, he asserted:

> Learned institutions ought to be favorite objects with every free people. They throw that light over the public mind, which is the best security against crafty and dangerous encroachments on the public liberty. They are nurseries of skillful teachers, for the schools distributed throughout the community. (Niles, 1822-1823)

Founding fathers such as Jefferson and Madison viewed the role of state government when it came to education as one of support, not accountability. It was assumed that teachers would effectively do the work of educating our children so that our republic would stay strong.

As our country grew, it experienced growing pains, and it also continued to rely on teachers as a national resource. During and after the Civil War, teachers were called upon to educate former slaves in how to be free citizens. For example, teachers contributed significantly to the Port Royal experiment. Port Royal was part of the Sea Islands off the coast of South Carolina that were captured by the Union army in 1861. Thousands of former slaves had gathered on the islands, and the U.S. government needed to attend to their needs (Goldstein, 2014). Edward Pierce, an attorney in charge of the experiment, sent out a call for teachers who would teach "important and fundamental lessons of civilization, —voluntary industry, self-reliance, frugality, fore-thought, honesty and truthfulness, cleanliness and order. With these will be combined intellectual, moral and religious instruction" (Chase, 1862, p. 36).

The Port Royal experiment and later efforts to educate former slaves helped to advance education throughout black communities, but racist policies culminating in the *Plessy v. Ferguson* decision kept black and white schools segregated, so almost 100 years later, teachers were again called into action. Attorney Thurgood Marshall and his colleagues argued in *Brown v. Board of Education of Topeka, Kansas*, that segregation itself, not just inequality in the schools, was unconstitutional based on the Fourteenth Amendment (Goldstein, 2014). Although many fought the ruling—including those using "naked racist political tactics...that fought desegregation in large part by attacking veteran black educators" (Goldstein, 2014, pp. 111-112)—teachers of all races stepped up to advance the larger issue of equal rights by welcoming *all* students, regardless of race, into their classrooms. Section 504 of the Rehabilitation Act of 1973 expanded this fight against discrimination to individuals with disabilities, and teachers were again on the front lines as they welcomed students with disabilities into their classrooms as well.

In 1965, President Lyndon B. Johnson pulled teachers into his "War on Poverty" with the passing of the Elementary and Secondary Education Act (ESEA), which provided funding to poor schools (through Title I) with the expectation that the additional funds would help these schools better meet the needs of our poorest children. Johnson stated in his remarks while signing ESEA into law (in his hometown in Texas, with one of his own elementary teachers by his side), "As the son of a tenant farmer, I know that education is only valid in its passport from poverty, the only valid passport. As a former teacher—and I hope a future one—I have great expectations of what this law will mean for all our young people" (Goldstein, 2014, p. 114). The nation had just entrusted teachers with fixing the educational gap created by poverty.

I've only included a few examples here, but from the founding of our nation through each phase of its growth, teachers have willingly responded to the calls to action as a valuable resource to lead the change in fixing society's problems. There were no external metrics on teacher effectiveness during any of these efforts. No sanctions. No incentives. Teachers shut their doors and focused on the Big Three, and we trusted them, even depended on them, to do so.

BALANCE BASED ON TRUST

Throughout my first year of teaching, I was keenly aware of my own shortcomings. As I reflected on that first year, I was grateful for the struggle; I had learned a lot. Year two was going to be different. I was quick to establish routines and found it much easier to implement sound classroom management strategies that worked for me. I knew where I wanted to go and devised a simple strategy to make it happen.

I began the year with a mindset of keeping things simple. Each day, I had a very clear and organized schedule with consistent classroom routines. It didn't take long for my students and me to settle in. My goal for the year was to move away from a rather traditional classroom environment toward a project-based one. I had hoped to do the same my first year but had rushed the process and failed miserably. This year, I was committed to making it happen slowly.

It started with a simple art project. I gave each student a picture that I had copied onto grid paper. Using the grid as a guide, the students had to replicate the picture on a plain piece of grid paper. We did this two or three times before I modified the activity to include a picture that was divided into two sections. Students were asked to work in pairs. One would re-create the top half of the picture, and the other would re-create the bottom half. The students would then align the two sections, creating one complete picture. Our first attempt left much to be desired. More often than not, the two sections didn't align. One or both of the students may have made their half of the picture too large or too small, and the results were less than optimal. Eventually, the students figured out that they could get together prior to starting their drawings and find the places where the two sections intersected. The students realized that when they worked together the results were better. I eventually had the students working in groups of four, and I also upped the difficulty level. Students were asked to translate the drawings using graph paper that was four times larger than the one found on the drawing. The students loved this activity. They saw it as an art project and naturally learned to work incredibly well together.

We finally moved to a whole-class project where I'd assigned each student a single section or two from the picture and asked them to translate it to a single 8"x 8" square on the grid. The results were massive images that stretched floor to ceiling. It was amazing to watch the students working together as they found the classmates who had adjacent squares and carefully calculated all of the intersecting points. They would make sure that each student was using the right color of crayon for the section and that each was applying the color in the same direction. This was the beginning of our move to a project-based learning environment. The students had learned to work together and were committed to doing their part to ensure the project was done well.

Over the course of the year, I began to integrate projects into academic areas. I began by assigning a single project to the entire class. Students were asked to work together in pairs, and each pair completed the project. Later, I would give the students two options. Each team would decide which project they wanted to complete and work together to do so. Over the course of several months, these project options and team makeups evolved. The projects became interdisciplinary, and students were able to select from a list of ten or fifteen projects. I gave students the option to work in teams of any size, but each week they had to select a completely new team.

The results were amazing. Each project had a clear set of objectives and guidelines. Each student had equal and defined responsibilities, and each group was responsible for grading their own project. I could always override the students' grades, but I found that the students were most often harder on themselves than I would have been. The bulk of our afternoons were devoted to projects. The students looked forward to that time and, without exception, worked harder and were on task more during project time. The students nearly always exceeded the parameters of the projects and displayed an element of creativity I hadn't planned for when I designed the projects.

Each Friday we gathered together, and the teams shared their project with the class. When students created picture books, they shared them with the kindergarten or first-grade students. They performed their plays for other classes and were more than willing to share their projects with anyone willing to listen. Students captured every project on video and maintained a video portfolio that grew throughout the year.

This style of teaching worked for me. It certainly doesn't work for everyone. I share this only to illustrate a point: I am not sure I would be able to implement this in my classroom if I was teaching in 2015. I was given a lot of autonomy and trust when I was teaching. I wasn't worried about making AYP or having my test scores posted in the local newspaper. I wasn't worried about being labeled a failure by the end-of-level tests, and I wasn't worried about getting a pay raise based on my students' performance on that test. I was worried about learning in the broadest sense of the word. If learning had been narrowed to how well my students performed on the math and language arts tests at the end of the year and the stakes were as high as they are today, I am not sure I would be willing to risk my future on project-based learning.

THE SWINGING PENDULUM

John Dewey hit the nail on the head when he said, "Mankind likes to think in terms of extreme opposites. It is given to formulating its beliefs in terms of *Either-Ors*, between which it recognizes no intermediate possibilities" (Dewey, 1938, p. 17). Public education isn't immune to this. It tends to swing back and forth between traditional and progressive philosophies on a pretty regular basis, although many don't seem to remember that it had visited the other end of the spectrum before. It reminds me of the resurgence of old songs and clothing styles, that none but the "wiser" (old) among us can remember.

This swing was happening in the 1960s and early 1970s as schools embraced the idea of open education (Cuban, 2004). Open education, although it goes by many names depending on when the pendulum swings its direction, has its roots in Dewey's idea of progressive education: a culture of individuality, free activity, learning through experience, and the connection between education and personal experience (Dewey, 1938). This style of education worked because up to this point, teachers were trusted, and so there was balance. As the decade progressed, however, public sentiment about education began to shift. For more than two centuries teachers had been seen as a national resource in helping the United States through its growing pains. But this view was about to be turned on its head because if teachers could help fix America, they could help break it, too.

Although the swing began in the late 1970s, it came into its own in the early 1980s with Reagan's appointment of Terrel (Ted) Bell as the secretary of education. Bell and Reagan were in many ways on opposite ends of the education spectrum. Bell had supported the bill to create the department of education; Reagan wanted to dismantle it (Gardner, 2005). But both were reasonable men, and both had their reasons for supporting the appointment, so Bell got the job.

Bell was aware of people's growing unease about the then-current state of education, as typified by declining student test scores and lax high school graduation requirements (Gardner, 2005). Because of this growing unease, Bell appointed a commission to review the state of America's schools. The commission included members who would lend credibility to the report's findings, including university presidents and professors (one of whom was also a Nobel laureate), members of state boards of education, principals, and the National Teacher of the Year for 1981–1982 (National Commission on Excellence in Education, 1983). Bell hoped to have the commission appointed by President Reagan but couldn't get anywhere with the administration, so he appointed them himself and directed the group to examine the quality of education in the United States and make recommendations (Gardner, 2005). The commission studied papers, meetings, analyses, letters, and other documents for the following eighteen months and in 1983 presented Bell with their results.

A Nation at Risk: The Imperative for Educational Reform begins with a sobering assessment:

> Our Nation is at risk. Our once unchallenged preeminence in commerce, industry, science, and technological innovation is being overtaken by competitors throughout the world. This report is concerned with only

one of the many causes and dimensions of the problem, but it is the one that undergirds American prosperity, security, and civility.... The educational foundations of our society are presently being eroded by a rising tide of mediocrity that threatens our very future as a Nation and a people. What was unimaginable a generation ago has begun to occur—others are matching and surpassing our educational attainments. (National Commission on Excellence in Education, 1983)

That phrase, "rising tide of mediocrity," and the bleak landscape it painted of eroding American competitiveness, captured people's imaginations. Fear can be quite compelling. The report went on to compare the United States (unfavorably) to Japanese, South Korean, and German efficiency and asserted that "learning is the indispensable investment required for success in the 'information age' we are entering" (National Commission on Excellence in Education, 1983). It also cited low international test scores, adult illiteracy, declining SAT scores, and increases in college remedial courses among its "Indicators of the Risk" (National Commission on Excellence in Education, 1983).

Bell established the commission in order to provide recommendations to schools, but as Diane Ravitch (2010) points out, "[The report] was notable for what it did not say" (p. 25). It refers to grades, high school graduation requirements, curriculum, college admissions requirements, and standardized assessments of achievement that "should be administered at major transition points from one level of schooling to another and particularly from high school to college or work" (National Commission on Excellence in Education, 1983). But it doesn't refer to high-stakes accountability anywhere. It doesn't even include the words *accountable* and *accountability*. It does recommend that "citizens across the Nation hold educators and elected officials responsible for providing the leadership necessary to achieve these reforms," but it also recommends "citizens provide the fiscal support and stability required to bring about the reforms we propose" (National Commission on Excellence in Education, 1983). High-stakes accountability using standardized testing is nowhere to be found in this report.

What it did do, though, was create through its rhetoric a sentiment of fear and solidify a new set of growing assumptions about education. Until this point, the prevailing attitude about public education was that it was a national resource, a public good that could be leveraged to address social and economic challenges in this country. The assumption was that America was great, in large part, because America was educated. And teachers were trusted to do the educating. The new assumptions erased the nation's trust in our public schools—and by default in our teachers—and replaced trust with fear.

Society had not yet swung all the way from trust in teachers to trust in testing and external, high-stakes accountability, but the pendulum wasn't done swinging yet.

DO YOU HAVE KIDS?

"Do you have kids?" I was initially surprised by how often parents would ask me this question. It always struck me as a little too personal and a bit passive aggressive. I believed they were questioning my ability to understand the needs of their child simply because

I didn't have children. It typically came up during parent-teacher conferences and was often coupled with a discussion about their child's unique needs. I always reassured them that I truly understood their concerns and would do everything I possibly could to help their child succeed. I cared about my students, and I really couldn't see how being a parent would change that.

My son was born on August 31, 1999. Ironically, it happened to be the very first day of school and my first day on the job as a middle school assistant principal. I had never worked in a middle school before and had fretted over the first day for several weeks. I woke up to a beautiful late-summer morning and rushed out the door to ensure an early arrival. I have always loved the nervous but excited energy that fills a school on the first day. I remember feeling surprisingly calm as I entered the school.

As I opened the door to my new office, the phone was already ringing. "Good morning, this is Mr. Goble. How can I help you?" I was surprised to hear, "This is your wife, my water just broke, and you need to come and take me to the hospital." I had been planning for a hectic first day on the job, but this was a bit of a shock. I quickly raced out of the building, and before I knew it, we were at the hospital. Amy was in labor fourteen hours before Elliot finally decided to make his entry into our lives. Looking at him for the first time, I had a new appreciation for why parents so often asked me if I had children. Having a child absolutely changed the way I viewed the world and more specifically changed the way I viewed education. From nearly the first moment I held Elliot in my arms, I began to worry about his future. I worried about his safety, I worried about his health, I worried about his development, and I worried that I might not be able to protect him.

Like all parents, we noticed his every milestone achievement and wondered how he compared to his peers. He began walking at ten months. That seemed above average. He began speaking at an early age—that was surely a sign of giftedness. We read to him for what seemed like hours every day. We were overly enamored by his progress and completely consumed with helping him learn and grow. For the first eighteen months of Elliot's life, he was the absolute center of our world.

Our daughter was born in March of 2001. Much to my surprise, Maggie was very different from Elliot. She would fall fast asleep the moment we placed her in her crib, whereas Elliot required an exhausting routine of rocking, reading, and singing before carefully placing him in his crib. Maggie was easy-going and highly adventurous, while Elliot was serious and inquisitive. Maggie loved to sing and dance, while Elliot preferred shooting hoops in the living room. It was humbling to realize Maggie and Elliot were not just byproducts of the parenting we were providing them; rather, they were two entirely unique people with individual personalities, talents, interests, and needs that came with them into our family, independent of anything Amy or I had done.

While they were very different in many ways, there were many similarities, too. Maggie walked at ten months and would sit in our laps for hours while we read her favorite books. They both devoured every *Magic Tree House* book in sequence, and Elliot's love of Harry Potter was eventually surpassed by Maggie's obsession. As parents, we have always considered ourselves lucky to have two amazing kids. It is a joy to watch them grow and evolve into complex individuals. Much of their growth can be attributed to amazing teachers who have helped them see the world from different perspectives.

"Do you have kids?" When Elliot and Maggie started school, I was able to better understand why parents asked me this question. Sending your kids off to school is scary. You can't help but worry. I have never asked that question of my children's teachers, but I can see what those parents were really trying to say. They were really saying, "I need you to understand that my child is the most important thing in the world to me, and I need to know that you care. I need you to see in her what I see. I need you to know that I worry about her safety. I want her to fit in with the other kids. I pray that you will lift her up when she falls down. I want her to be excited to go to school every day, and I want her talents to be nurtured and her weaknesses to be strengthened. I just wanted to know if you have kids because if you do, you will know why I asked. You will understand that I am entrusting you with the thing I value the most in the world—my child."

TO NCLB AND BEYOND

A Nation at Risk solidified a growing doubt in society's minds around the effectiveness of our schools.

Before, when society viewed teachers as a national resource, accountability was local. Parents held teachers accountable for the safety and learning of their children, but this accountability was based on trust, not doubt. Teachers' artifacts of accountability, such as syllabi, were directed to parents, students, and principals. Teachers didn't have any other artifacts—they didn't need them. Parents trusted teachers to do their jobs and keep their children safe.

When the pendulum began to swing and society began to doubt instead of trust, teachers were unprepared to show accountability in any significant way other than through the students they taught, and policymakers were unprepared to demand accountability in any other way, as well. It was on this foundation—this vacuum of documented accountability—that national interests began to build the external, high-stakes accountability we have today.

In the wake of *A Nation at Risk*, there was near universal consensus across political parties that the time had come for government to take a more active role in ensuring that our schools were up to par. But that didn't mean that ubiquitous testing and high-stakes accountability showed up right away. *A Nation at Risk* hadn't indicted teachers. But it did imply that all was not well with teachers in three areas: (1) teachers are "beleaguered," and various efforts should be made to ease their burden; (2) teacher preparation programs need to do a better job of preparing teachers; and (3) teaching needs to be a more rewarding and respected profession. (There are many references to teachers within the report, but none are condemning of them. For examples, see pages 12, 22, 29–30 and "Recommendation D: Teaching," beginning on page 30 of *A Nation at Risk*.)

A Nation at Risk's primary focus was on the underperformance of our nation's high schools. The report includes in its introduction the following statement: "The Commission's charter directed it to pay particular attention to teenage youth, and we have done so largely by focusing on high schools" (National Commission on Excellence in Education, 1983). The report includes very little information about elementary or middle schools. It includes only one elementary-level finding, and the only recommendation directed specifically to elementaries is to begin teaching foreign language (National Commission on Excellence in Education, 1983).

Armed with this relatively scant information, states began looking into how they could help schools improve. But where to begin? *A Nation at Risk* (National Commission on Excellence in Education, 1983) had made five recommendations:

- **RECOMMENDATION A:** Strengthen state and local high school graduation requirements.

- **RECOMMENDATION B:** Adopt more rigorous and measurable standards, higher expectations for academic performance and student conduct, and stricter requirements for college admission.

- **RECOMMENDATION C:** Provide more time for learning.

- **RECOMMENDATION D:** Make teaching a more rewarding and respected profession.

- **RECOMMENDATION E:** Expect society to hold educators and politicians responsible for providing necessary leadership to "achieve these reforms" and be willing to pay for the reforms that educators and politicians implement.

Recommendation A was relatively easy—high schools around the nation began to strengthen requirements for graduation. Recommendation B inspired our entire movement of standards-based education reform and the standardized testing that would go with it. Recommendation C was hard. It would cost money and time and restructuring to get it right, so any serious attempts to implement it were largely avoided. Recommendation D resulted in some additional or alternate requirements to become teachers, as well as some merit-pay attempts that kind of fizzled over time (Goldstein, 2014). But recommendation E was key, because it gave permission for politicians to move from the role of offering support to one of ensuring accountability.

In September of 1989, President George H. W. Bush, building on educational reform momentum in states such as Tennessee and Arkansas, organized a National Educational Summit in Charlottesville, Virginia, to discuss ideas about reforming public education (New York State Archives, n.d.). Bush, along with governors from forty-nine states, business leaders, and Cabinet members discussed educational goals. Bush also made it clear that he was not there to establish a federal role in any solution—just to provide support. Education was still a matter for the states.

Governor Clinton of Arkansas played a key role in the summit, which eventually led to a set of national goals for public education. The following January, Bush (1990) read the six national goals, endorsed by the coalition of governors, in his State of the Union address:

○ By the year 2000, every child must start school ready to learn.

○ The United States must increase the high school graduation rate to no less than 90 percent.

○ And we are going to make sure our schools' diplomas mean something. In critical subjects—at the fourth, eighth, and twelfth grades—we must assess our students' performance.

○ By the year 2000, U.S. students must be first in the world in math and science achievement.

○ Every American adult must be a skilled, literate worker and citizen.

○ Every school must offer the kind of disciplined environment that makes it possible for our kids to learn. And every school in America must be drug-free.

If we read carefully, we can see a subtle shift toward external accountability along with the efforts around higher expectations as recommended in *A Nation at Risk*. Every child *must* start school ready to learn. We are going to *make sure* our schools' diplomas mean something. We *must* assess our students' performance. The National Assessment for Educational Progress (NAEP), a norm-referenced, standardized test in use since 1969, was still voluntary at this point. (Technically federal law still indicates that the NAEP is voluntary, but NCLB tied Title I funds to the requirement to participate in the NAEP for fourth and eighth grades reading and math [National Center for Education Statistics, n.d.b].) But the pendulum wasn't done swinging.

The following year, Bush again presented the six goals (which had been a bit spruced up) as a "long-term national strategy," in part to encourage Congress to pass the AMERICA 2000 Excellence in Education Act (U.S. Department of Education, 1991). The act didn't pass, but on page 33 of the sourcebook is some foreshadowing of future directions: most notably, the federal government rewarding progress and spurring change. And the pendulum still wasn't done swinging.

Bill Clinton had been deeply involved in the creation of the AMERICA 2000 goals, so it made sense that he would continue on that path once he became president. Clinton expanded on the six original goals and added two more:

○ By the year 2000, the Nation's teaching force will have access to programs for the continued improvement of their professional skills and the opportunity to acquire the knowledge and skills needed to instruct and prepare all American students for the next century.

○ By the year 2000, every school will promote partnerships that will increase parental involvement and participation in promoting the social, emotional, and academic growth of children. (United States of America 103d Congress, 1993)

The Goals 2000: Educate America Act was signed into law in March of 1994. It was boldly ideal. Some of the expanded goals hearkened back to Johnson's

War on Poverty: "children will receive the nutrition, physical activity experiences, and health care needed to arrive at school with healthy minds and bodies" (United States of America 103d Congress, 1993). Others foreshadowed No Child Left Behind: "the academic performance of all students at the elementary and secondary level will increase significantly in every quartile, and the distribution of minority students in each quartile will more closely reflect the student population as a whole" (United States of America 103d Congress, 1993). It even gave a nod to the increasing presence of business in education: "partnerships will be established, whenever possible, among local educational agencies...and...business...to provide and support programs for the professional development of educators" (United States of America 103d Congress, 1993). When we look back at the goals in this act, we can see that the shift from trust to accountability wasn't complete, but we also see that teachers were firmly in the need-to-fix category.

Later that same year, Congress took up the scheduled reauthorization of Johnson's Elementary and Secondary Education Act (ESEA). Congress periodically modernizes laws to reflect societal changes, and when they do, they must reauthorize the law (National School Boards Association, n.d.). This presented the Clinton administration with the opportunity to influence school reform efforts in a beefier way than with the Goals 2000 Act.

The successful reauthorization, titled Improving America's Schools Act (IASA), included requirements for states to create state-level standards, define annual yearly progress, and develop or adopt yearly student assessments. But more important, it finally shifted the balance from trust to accountability—although the accountability wasn't yet directly tied to teachers—when it tied the state's ability to receive Title I funding to these measures. One of Johnson's key programs in his War on Poverty had just been appropriated as a means of enforcing local compliance with federally mandated goals.

States began working to meet the requirements of IASA, and a patchwork of accountability measures began to take shape across the country. Almost everyone was on board with the basic premises found in the law (National Center for Education Statistics, 2003).

But by the year 2000, none of Bush's original six goals had been met:

- **EARLY CHILDHOOD SCHOOL READINESS:** Although the percentage of children who lived in families with incomes below the poverty level fell 1.7 percent between 1989 and 1999, 16 percent of America's children still lived in poverty (Johnson, Kominski, Smith, & Tillman, 2005).

- **HIGH SCHOOL GRADUATION:** 85.9 percent of adults ages eighteen to twenty-four had completed high school (National Center for Education Statistics, 2000).

- **STUDENT ASSESSMENT:** Ten states tested students in elementary, middle, and high school in the subjects of math, language arts, science, and social studies. (If you only count math and language arts the number jumps to thirty-four.) (National Center for Education Statistics, 2003).

- **INTERNATIONAL ACHIEVEMENT:** U.S. students ranked eighteenth in math and fourteenth in science achievement on the 2000 Program for International Student Assessment (PISA) (National Center for Education Statistics, 2001)

○ **ADULT LITERACY:** Approximately 86 percent of American adults had at least a basic level of literacy (National Center for Education Statistics, n.d.a).

○ **SCHOOL SAFETY:** 71 percent of public schools experienced at least one violent incident, and 27 percent of schools experienced at least one incident of possession or use of alcohol or illegal drugs (National Center for Education Statistics, 2005).

Accountability didn't seem to be budging things much, but the decade was still young.

George W. Bush said he was running for president because he wanted "to help usher in the responsibility era, where people understand they are responsible for the choice they make and are held accountable for their actions" (4President Corporation, n.d.). His vision to improve education included school choice, character education, local control, rewards for success, and sanctions for failure (4President Corporation, n.d.). After a *very* close race (and some recounts and a lawsuit), Bush took office and appointed Rod Paige as the U.S. secretary of education. The appointment of Paige was significant because he had been the Houston school superintendent who was credited with the

"Texas Miracle," and Bush modeled his reauthorization of ESEA in part on this "miracle" (Leung, 2004).

Bush drew elements from Clinton's IASA—the disaggregation of data by demographics, the linking of federal funding to federal requirements—and combined them with Paige's ideas around accountability to create the No Child Left Behind Act of 2001 (NCLB). The provisions of this law are probably better known than any other piece of federal legislation. The law requires schools to administer annual standardized tests in math and language arts for grades 3–8 and for one grade in high school. And the results of these annual exams are to be used almost exclusively to determine the success or failure of schools (United States of America 107th Congress, 2002). Ninety-five percent of all students are required to take the exam for the school to receive a passing grade. Year over year, improvement must be shown, along with increased graduation rates and one other metric, such as student attendance. State agencies are required to submit plans that met these stringent criteria (United States of America 107th Congress, 2002).

NCLB is nothing if not detailed on the enforcement end. Schools that don't meet adequate early progress (AYP) move through a series of increasingly painful sanctions, and although teachers aren't individually targeted by these sanctions, many of the sanctions require that teachers get fired if schools don't meet AYP (United States of America 107th Congress, 2002).

The pendulum was almost there. Bush's reauthorization of Johnson's ESEA—about which Johnson (1965) assured members of Congress, "Federal assistance does not mean federal control"—was the most dramatic imposition of federal control on state and local public education in the history of our nation. But one requirement in particular of this law doomed it to failure and provided opportunity for the pendulum to finish its swing.

NCLB included within its vast number of pages one small paragraph:

> **IN GENERAL** – Each local educational agency plan shall provide assurances that the local educational agency will use the results of

> the student academic assessments required under section 1111(b)(3), and other measures or indicators available to the agency, to review annually the progress of each school served by the agency and receiving funds under this part to determine whether all of the schools are making the progress necessary to ensure that all students will meet the State's proficient level of achievement on the State academic assessments described in section 1111(b)(3) within 12 years from the end of the 2001-2002 school year. (United States of America 107th Congress, 2002)

OK, nothing written by the government is *small*. In English, this is the section that requires 100 percent proficiency by the end of the 2013–2014 school year. This was, of course, an impossible goal. And as 2014 got closer and closer, it became clearer and clearer that most schools were going to fail.

In 2011, the Obama administration (Bush was long gone by now):

> invited each State Education Agency (SEA) to request flexibility regarding specific require-ments of the No Child Left Behind Act of 2001 (NCLB) in exchange for rigorous and com-prehensive State-developed plans designed to improve educational outcomes for all students, close achievement gaps, increase equity, and improve the quality of instruction. (U.S. Department of Education, 2012)

States were being asked to rob Peter in order to pay Paul in return for waivers on twelve NCLB requirements, including the 100 percent proficiency requirement. Schools and districts would now have to implement teacher and principal evaluation systems that included "as a significant factor data on student growth for all students (including English Learn-ers and students with disabilities)" (U.S. Department of Education, 2012). The Obama administration had used incentives to promote policies before. In 2009, when states were struggling financially, it offered Race to the Top grants that gave points for adopting "a common set of high-quality standards" (i.e., the Com-mon Core) (U.S. Department of Education, 2009).

Cash-strapped states adopted the standards in order to be able to *apply* for the grants, without any guarantee they would actually receive funding. As NCLB began to slowly strangle schools with its rigid requirements, states willingly adopted the devil they did not know—and the pendulum finally hit the wall.

Over the course of a mere thirty years, society went from trusting our teachers to applying external, high-stakes, *individual* accountability for someone else's work—proof of professionalism based largely on only one element of the Big Three: identifying student levels of understanding as measured by a single test score.

CHAPTER 2

SEARCHING FOR BALANCE

OUR THIRTY-YEAR TREK TO EXTERNAL, HIGH-STAKES, INDIVIDUAL ACCOUNTABILITY has left us with paradoxes that illustrate why we need to search for balance. I include here two examples found among the many criteria teachers use daily to help inform and evaluate their application of the Big Three: (1) the paradox of teaching to standards and (2) the paradox of measuring student achievement.

The standard paradox. Every industry has standards. Education's primary standards are academic standards, of which the most familiar sets are math and English language arts as outlined in the Common Core State Standards (CCSS). When it comes to standards, the Common Core has pretty much sucked all of the oxygen out of the room. I'm not going to weigh in on the politics of the CCSS here (that's another book). I mention them only as an example of these academic standards. Many noneducators may be surprised to learn that nearly *every* area of study, from pottery to chemistry to animal husbandry, has a set of standards. In cases where standards don't exist, teachers usually create them. Standards represent the desired learning outcomes for any area of study.

Teachers most often align their implementation of the Big Three elements to academic standards associated with the courses they teach, as these standards provide natural criteria for accountability. But teachers are also urged, and sometimes required, to focus on instructional shifts such as those associated with the Common Core. These shifts encourage deeper learning and more complex thinking from students, as exemplified by the math shift of greater focus on fewer topics (National Governors Association Center for Best Practices and Council of Chief State School Officers, n.d.).

These strategies also take *time*. Complex learning, like complex teaching, is a process that takes time to develop. But just as we've begun to emphasize complex teaching and learning in the form of the Common Core's instructional shifts, we've also created so many standards that teachers end up teaching a mile wide and an inch deep. For example, the Common Core math standards, with their emphasis on fewer topics, include twenty-nine sixth-grade standards, but if you consider that some of these standards include multiple subcomponents, then there are forty-two concepts. Teachers must ensure students gain a deep, foundational knowledge of these forty-two concepts over the course of the year. This number doesn't sound like much until we remember that *every* subject has academic standards teachers must ensure students are gaining a deep, foundational knowledge of. Multiply forty-two by four (assuming students are learning the four core subjects of math, English language arts, science, and social studies), and teachers must address an average of either 168 different concepts to 30 different students or 42 concepts to 150 different students, all in the course of 180 days. And this doesn't take into consideration the time taken by the *other* subjects such as foreign language, the arts, physical education, and so on, or the time teachers must devote to testing and test preparation. Teachers are expected to provide rich, meaningful learning experiences for our children around hundreds of standards or with hundreds of students.

The achievement paradox. Standards aren't the only criteria where we find paradoxes. We find them in our approaches to measuring student achievement as well. The U.S. Department of Education (n.d.) advocates personalized learning as leading "to better student outcomes because the pace of learning is customized to each student." But No Child Left Behind requires that student achievement is determined by professional assessment standards and "based on the appropriate level of subject matter knowledge for grade levels to be assessed, or the age of the students, as the case may be" (United States of America 107th Congress, 2002). The Race to the Top program modifies the NCLB requirement somewhat by introducing the concept of student growth, but it also expects a highly qualified teacher to produce high rates of student growth and provides an example of this growth as "one and one-half grade levels in an academic year" (U.S. Department of Education, 2009). Teachers are encouraged (and sometimes required) to personalize student learning for anywhere between 30 and 150 students, while at the same time being evaluated by student outcomes that are all generated on the same day.

These two paradoxes illustrate how unbalanced our educational system has become. It is in the wake of these and other educational paradoxes that we begin our search for balance in the areas of support, measures, people, and market-based reform.

BALANCE OF SUPPORT

Sometime around 2012, I began to notice that teacher resignation letters were going viral on the Internet in blogs, articles, and videos. Teachers in every state were announcing in a very public way their dissatisfaction with a job they once loved. They were admitting that they had been stretched too far and were finally broken. The common theme of these letters seemed to center around the increasing volume of high-stakes testing (and preparation for high-stakes testing), unrealistic expectations, loss of autonomy, increasing demands, and the lack of support from central leadership. These were teachers who passionately declared their love of teaching while admitting that love and passion were not enough to keep them in the profession that no longer seemed to value them.

Susan Sluyter, a kindergarten teacher from Massachusetts, wrote an impassioned letter of resignation highlighted in the *Washington Post* that started out with a sentiment felt by many teachers:

> In this disturbing era of testing and data collection in the public schools, I have seen my career transformed into a job that no longer fits my understanding of how children learn and what a teacher ought to do in the classroom to build a healthy, safe, developmentally appropriate environment for learning for each of our children. I have experienced, over the past few years, the same mandates that all teachers in the district have experienced. I have watched as my job requirements swung away from a focus on the children, their individual learning styles, emotional needs, and their individual families, interests and strengths to a focus on testing, assessing, and scoring young children, thereby ramping

> up the academic demands and pressures on them. (Strauss, 2014)

Kris L. Nielsen, a teacher in North Carolina, is another who crafted his resignation and had it show up on Diane Ravitch's blog and the *Washington Post*. In his letter, he shares his many frustrations with a system that had grown to be unbearable:

> I refuse to subject students to every ridiculous standardized test that the state and/or district thinks is important. I refuse to have my higher-level and deep thinking lessons disrupted by meaningless assessments (like the EXPLORE test) that do little more than increase stress among children and teachers, and attempt to guide young adolescents into narrow choices. (Strauss, 2014)

Gary Wiener from New York wrote about the ten reasons he was retiring after thirty years in an article found on *The Week*. It was a mostly humorous take on the challenges and annoyances experienced by teachers, but number seven provided insight into the loss of trust many teachers feel when it comes to evaluating their students' performance:

On June 20, I spent the day scoring the English Language Arts Regents Exam, a New York state comprehensive test that functions as a graduation requirement. My colleagues informed me that my students wrote great essays. Too bad I wasn't allowed to read them. (Teachers can no longer score their own students' exams.) (Wiener, 2014)

I believe Sluyter's final sentence in her letter of resignation best captures the sentiments of a large number of teachers who feel the teaching profession has changed in ways that make leaving preferable to staying:

> I felt I needed to survive by looking elsewhere and leaving the community I love so dearly. I did not feel I was leaving my job. I felt then and feel now that my job left me. (Strauss, 2014)

The letters are usually accompanied with comments from fellow teachers who share their appreciation and support. Many share stories of similar frustrations or admit to having recently resigned or retired for the very same reasons. Reading these letters made me think of a scene from the movie *The Goonies*. Some may remember *The Goonies* as a 1980s Steven Spielberg adventure movie where a wealthy land developer threatens to demolish an entire coastal neighborhood to build a golf course. The preteen central characters Mikey, Mouth, and Data find a treasure map hidden on the back of a picture stored in the attic of Mikey's home. The scene begins after the boys, Mikey's older brother, and two teenage girls have set out on a treacherous journey through caves once used by pirates to store their treasure. The kids unknowingly find themselves sitting at the bottom of a wishing well strewn with coins. The pivotal moment in the scene is when Mouth displays anger and frustration toward a world that threatens to take away his home and his friends. Mikey, Mouth, and Data mistake the scattered coins for the treasure and begin to fill their pockets. When Stef, one of the older girls, realizes what is happening, she becomes upset and tells them to stop:

> Stef: Wait, wait, you can't do this.
>
> Data: Why?
>
> Mikey: Why?
>
> Stef: Because, these are somebody else's wishes. They're somebody else's dreams.
>
> Mouth: Yeah, but you know what? This one, this one right here, this was my dream, my wish—and it didn't come true. So I'm taking it back, I'm taking them all back. (Donner, 1985)

Many teachers enter the teaching profession with a simple desire to help children learn and grow. They have dreams of making a difference, of giving back and doing their part to make the lives of children a little better. The decision to become a teacher is rarely based on dreams of high, future salaries or job promotions. For many, NCLB represented a threat to their profession. It was the wealthy land developer who wanted to tear down their neighborhood in favor of a new golf course. This realization has left many teachers feeling a lot like

Mouth, their dreams of making a difference were shattered and the only recourse they felt they had was to leave. The education profession cannot afford to lose any more teachers. We need to take back what is ours; we need to reclaim our wishes and dreams. We need to reclaim our classrooms.

I could relate to those letters. I had spent my entire administrative career working as a principal in a large (over 70,000 students), rapidly growing school district. Nearly all of the growth was occurring on the west side of the district, requiring the district to build one or two new schools each year just to keep up. Many argued that the older schools on the east side were not receiving the necessary upgrades or maintenance as a result. This, along with the perception that the massive size of the district limited adequate input from all stakeholders, caused the east-side patrons to propose dividing the district along east and west lines. New state laws allowed for the division and limited voting to those communities who proposed the split. In a very close vote of east-side residences, two new districts were formed.

During the interim period before the split was official, a new board was created, and a new superintendent and an entirely new district administration and staff had to be hired. Throughout the process, a new vision for the district was emerging, and I liked what I was hearing from the new superintendent. He talked of giving schools more autonomy and of giving teachers more of a voice in the decision-making process. He energized the community, and what he had to say appealed to me.

Several of my colleagues had called and encouraged me to apply for a district leadership position in the new district. My initial thought was that I wasn't interested. I had fallen in love with my current school. I worked with an amazing group of teachers and staff, and I loved the community and kids. Both of my own children attended the school, and I considered it a gift to have that time with them. But the allure of working in a district that wanted to listen to teachers and build a positive rapport between the central office and its schools was enough to get me to apply. In 2009, I accepted a position as a director of elementary schools. It felt like a once-in-a-lifetime opportunity, and I was excited to help start a brand-new district.

I loved my new role, and I relished the opportunity to support the schools under my supervision. My fellow school directors were also former employees of the original school district prior to the split, while many others on the leadership team were coming from surrounding districts. We had a few months to get ready for the transition from one district to two. During this time, there were countless planning meetings where we all got to know one another and the mood was generally optimistic. The school year began with celebrations, media coverage, and plenty of goodwill. As the newly branded buses arrived to drop students off for their first day of school, it became official—a new district was born.

Memories of those days seem almost surreal to me now. Over the course of the next few years, I found myself at odds with the direction the district was taking. The initial promises of giving schools more autonomy and listening to input from teachers gave way to a centralized vision. For the most part, the faculties and staff within the schools were far removed from the politics that had created the district and unaware of the changes being proposed at the central office. Many within the district had seen the split as a mandate for change and an admission that the methods being used by teachers prior to the split were in need of an immediate overhaul. Having worked in the district prior to the split, I felt responsible for helping those who had come from other districts better understand the previous culture and for mitigating the possible conflicts that might arise as we developed a new one.

In my role as a school supervisor, I was fielding calls from teachers and principals who expressed concerns that they were being left out of the conversation. They had been led to believe that decisions would be made with their input, and that wasn't happening. I initially expressed my apprehension about the lack of input we were receiving from schools. Over time, it became clear, however, that the perception of dissent or unease around the decisions being made by those above me was not going to be tolerated by the new administration. I felt caught between a rock and a hard place. I could keep my mouth shut and curry favor with my superiors, or I could continue to advocate for the teachers and principals I was assigned to support. I had lost faith in my superiors, and they had lost faith in me.

For the first time in my career, I began to dread going to work. Teaching had been a labor of love, and for the most part, the daily decisions of how to best meet the needs of my students were left to me. I have often said that the best job in education is the elementary school principal. I loved working with and supporting teachers. I loved the opportunity to become part of a community. I embraced the challenges, and most of all, I loved being around the children. They were a daily reminder that the work we did every day mattered. I had been unprepared for the politics of working in a district office. I didn't belong there. I realized my decision to go to the district office was as much about my ego and a salary increase as it was about helping others.

I doubt seriously the politics and frustrations I felt in the district office were any different than I would have experienced in most other districts. It certainly isn't uncommon for district offices to become shrouded in a bubble that filters out the daily issues facing teachers. For the most part, schools have used the distance between the district office and the school as a buffer from unrealistic and misguided mandates. As a principal, I was usually able to shield my teachers from the hyperbole and find ways to adhere to mandates without overwhelming them. I had assumed that I would be able to do the same for the principals I supervised—shield them from unrealistic and misguided mandates. This, however, wasn't really my job.

When I signed up to work in the district office, I had unknowingly switched teams. Early in my career as a principal, my boss and I were having a conversation in his office. I can remember him looking right at me with a serious look on his face as if he was debating whether or not to tell me what he was thinking. After a long pause he said, "I think you are going places, but if I had to do it all over again, if I knew then what I know now, I would never leave the school. You will never be in a better position to make a difference in the lives of children than you are now." It was wise counsel from someone who understood me and also knew that I probably wouldn't fully understand him until it was too late.

The most important work in education occurs in schools and, more specifically, in classrooms. There are countless educators who work tirelessly and with real purpose in district positions to support the teachers, administrators, and staff who carry out the important work of educating children. These are jobs that often require the skills of a politician. I didn't want to be a politician. I had not found the purpose I had hoped to find in the district office. It did, however, help me understand that my real purpose was to be in a school helping children and supporting those who endeavor every day to make a difference in their lives. I was eventually given the opportunity (which is a nice way of saying my boss came to the conclusion that we weren't on the same team) to return to the best job in education: elementary school principal.

There was a large part of me that felt fortunate to be working in a school again. It was exhilarating to be around the students, and I absolutely loved the faculty. I was, however, unable to avoid a nagging realization: it was getting harder to shelter the teachers from mandates that were clearly wearing on them. More tests were being mandated, and the pressure to focus on improving test scores was eclipsing our focus on meeting the complex and diverse needs of our students. I could feel the morale of teachers diminishing as their role began to devolve into data management. It would be hard to explain to anyone exactly why teachers were feeling overwhelmed or underappreciated because it wasn't just one thing. It was a little like dying from a thousand paper cuts. *A Nation at Risk*, No Child Left Behind, Race to the Top, the Common Core, education reform, school rankings, underfunding, growing class sizes, years without a pay increase, new methods, new materials, test-based accountability, and a myriad of other issues were conspiring against the claim teachers once had on their own classrooms.

MISSING THE FOREST FOR THE TREES

I've always liked to think of the school principal as an instructional leader whose job it is to help teachers become better teachers and to support parents and students in the whole process of learning. The derivation of the word *principal* comes from the fact that the school principal used to be the "principal teacher" in the school, in the same way that the "principal dancer" is the highest-ranking, most-experienced ballerina in a ballet company—a leader among peers (Head Teacher, n.d.). But over the years, principals have become more school managers than instructional leaders. They help manage the implementation of federal, state, and district-mandated programs. More and more, they don't set their own targets or chart their own objectives like they used to.

District offices have a huge impact on the day-to-day workings of a school. I recently attended an educational conference devoted to the theory and practice of collaborative teacher teams. During a break, I started talking with a middle school principal from Iowa. He was a true believer, thoroughly committed to the collaborative process. I asked him how the implementation of subject and grade-level teams was going in his district. Culture change can be a difficult thing.

"You want to know where we are in the process?" he asked, testing my level of interest. He raised his eyebrows. "Well, let's see...In the wake of the Sandy Hook school shooting tragedy we've been given new A.L.I.C.E. [alert, lockdown, inform, counter, evacuate] lockdown procedures to implement immediately and educate our parents about. The Iowa state legislature just passed new antibullying legislation that we're required to operationalize. Our district has a new CBE [competency-based education] initiative that's kind of throwing all our teachers for a loop. The state incented adoption of a standards-based grading initiative with extra money on the table, and since we're a 'do anything for a dollar district,' we've just begun migrating to new reporting. And now I'm informed by the district that our schools are behind the other districts in end-of-level testing and that my school, in particular, is a bad testing school and I'd better get my act together, which means trying to grapple with the latest state testing data and what to do with it. They moved the testing date for the Iowa grade-level test from the fall to February, and then from February to April under the premise that postponing the test date would help the students perform better (at least for one year, right?). So now I get the test results upon which my success or failure as a principal is being judged from the state in a nice tidy package on...guess what day? The last in-service day of the year as the teachers are packing up their stuff and heading out the door.

"The superintendent who has been handing all of this down is stepping down this summer and a new superintendent is coming in. The high school we feed our kids into is getting a new principal at the same time. I have no idea what their philosophies will be or whether they will support the collaborative process we've begun. It's squirrel-based leadership around here. so who knows what the next all-hands-on-deck initiative will be.

"So, where are we in the team-building process? Are we using data in our classrooms? Have we built formative assessments? The answer is no. We're at the stage of just trying to identify what the standards will be. We have Common Core State Standards +15 [15 percent customization] available to us in Iowa, but that's not good enough for our district. It's like we're in the mine, and there is shiny stuff all around, but we've got to do our own digging. Our district is developing its own standards. We haven't started building common formative assessments yet because we don't have common standards yet. Every year, they say they're going reduce the state and district initiatives, but it's a lie, it's all a lie."

And his was an affluent school. His story pales in comparison to the turbulence facing many of our inner-city schools that layer on state and federal school take-overs and mass firings. In 2013, for example, the city district of Philadelphia faced a budget shortfall of $300 million and responded by closing twenty-three inner-city schools and laying off 4,000 employees, including assistant principals, nurses, aides, and almost 700 teachers (Young, 2013).

In many parts of our country, district leaders have made an about-face. Instead of representing the teachers and students and their needs to the state and federal

government, they represent the state and federal mandates to the teachers and students.

Michelle Rhee, who served as the chancellor of the
Washington DC Public Schools from 2007 to 2010, is a
good example of a superintendent who seemed to see
her role not as one of support and nurturing for teachers
and schools, but of being the arbiter of accountability
(Bolduan, 2008). If a school was failing, she fired the
principal and fired the staff and closed the school if she
had to. She was on the cover of *TIME* magazine with
a broom, sweeping out the bad teachers (Twomey,
2008). The premise was that teachers were the problem and needed to be rooted out. Instead of taking a
proactive approach and saying, "Let's involve teachers
in our decision making process," or "Let me get some
time in the district to figure out what the real issues
are," and then "How do we allocate our resources to be
able to support schools and improve teachers?" Rhee
took the much simpler approach of looking at test data
and using that test data to determine who was not performing and therefore needed to go.

But does a superintendent's impact on the workings of
a school translate into better student learning? A recent

report from the Brookings Institute was the first significant multiyear study on the impact of superintendents
on student performance, as measured by end-of-level
test data. The researchers examined changes in district
leadership and superintendent-led reform efforts as
correlated to test scores in Florida and North Carolina
from 2000 to 2010. Here's what they found:

> Superintendents account for only a small
> fraction of a percent (0.3 percent) of student
> differences in achievement....Most differ-
> ences in student achievement are attributable
> to student characteristics....Teachers, who
> account for four percent of the variance in
> student achievement, are the most important
> influences on student achievement among
> the hierarchy of the other [school-related]
> variables we measure. (Chingos, Whitehurst,
> & Lindquist, 2014)

Teachers have the greatest impact on student achievement within the school setting. A principal's primary
role should be one of instructional support for teachers.
The role of district leadership should be one of support

for both. District offices have to allocate resources and make sure that legal requirements are met, but a good district office puts the development of teachers first.

A LETTER TO PRINCIPALS AND ADMINISTRATORS

Studies have shown that principals who create a culture of community and cooperation—who direct their focus toward meeting the needs of their teachers, not their supervisors—encourage greater motivation and instructional effectiveness (Waters, Marzano, & McNulty, 2003). I have found these claims to be true in my personal experience as a teacher, principal, and district administrator. Teachers must lead the change in our schools, but they can't do it alone. The culture of a school, largely dictated by its principal, determines to a great extent the ability of its teachers to thrive. Even though this book is for teachers, I believe so strongly in a principal's obligation to be an instructional leader, not just a school manager, that I've included a letter here directed to them as a gentle reminder about their important role in finding balance when it comes to support. It is my hope that principals and administrators who read this will take it to heart, and that teachers who read this will share it with their principals.

Dear Principals,

Don't just support your teachers—be present.

All organizations are constantly working to maintain their relevance within the community they serve. This need to grow and improve inevitably requires members of the organization to be open to frequent change, and change can be messy without enlightened leadership. Schools are notorious for being slow to change. This should come as no surprise, as too often change is driven from the top down. Teachers are rarely included in the decision-making process but are expected to fully implement whatever program, technology, or fad is being levied upon them. Most teachers are open to improvement and are committed to the potential for positive, foundational change but quickly tire of the rapid succession of the short-lived reform ideas thrust upon them. So, with willing teachers, what is the biggest difference between ideas that succeed and ideas that fall short of their intended goal? The answer is simple: leaders who are present!

Real change, change that lasts and makes a difference, depends on leaders who understand the importance of building a collaborative culture within their schools—a culture built on mutual respect and, most important, trust. In order for this to occur, teachers and staff must feel empowered to participate in the process and trust that their voices will be heard. When schools embrace this premise, when teachers and staff work collectively to combine resources and share their expertise, the opportunity for meaningful change increases dramatically. But before we get ahead of ourselves, it is worth noting one important fact: getting your teachers and staff to fully embrace real change isn't easy. If you are not thoughtful in your implementation strategies, you may underestimate or contribute to making the implementation process very hard for your schools to achieve.

Is there a difference between a leader who is supportive and a leader who is present, and does it matter? I believe it is the difference between good schools and great schools. To use a sports analogy, fans and cheerleaders are supportive of their team while coaches and players are present with their team. Leaders must be both supportive and, more important, present if they are going to have an impact on school and student outcomes. It is not enough to provide the cheering section. The work is too great and important to stand on the sidelines. You have to be willing to stand shoulder to shoulder with teachers—you must be present in order to lead.

I have outlined the history of what got us to where we are today. I have addressed the impact this has had on teachers in their classrooms. The simple truth is that none of what I have written matters unless there are administrators willing to advocate and be present for their teachers. Schools need leaders who are willing to support what is best for children. Turning our schools into test-prep factories that narrow the curriculum is not good for children, and it undermines the work of teachers. As Don DeLay (2008) said, "A school cannot be a good place for students if it is not a good place for teachers."

Schools are more than their test scores. A school that sacrifices the souls of its children in pursuit of higher test scores is a school without enlightened leadership. It is a school without a leader who is present. To be present is to know your students, it is to know your faculty and staff, and it is to know your community. A leader who is present understands that educating children is a complex task that requires teachers who have autonomy, mastery, and purpose. A leader who is present understands that a number 2 pencil and a bubble sheet are tools that will fail to capture the learning that matters most. They don't capture creativity, joy, or empathy for one another. They don't capture the moment when a child finally understands a skill or concept that had previously eluded him.

It is easy to lose sight of what it means to be present with your teachers. It is easier to be present in your office or in meetings. It is easier to be present for the paperwork that litters your desk. It is easier to be present for phone calls from parents and patrons. It is quite easy to invest so much of your time being present for everything else that you forget to be present for the people who matter most—your teachers and students. They need you. They need you to listen to their concerns, and they need you to understand that many of them are afraid. They are afraid of being honest and they are afraid of losing their jobs. They have seen what has happened to other teachers and leaders who spoke out. In many cases, they are afraid of you. They need you to understand that fear drives compliance, but only trust can drive change. Change comes from within. They don't need platitudes or condemnations; they need you to be presentI have had the distinct pleasure to work with schools all over the country and have witnessed firsthand the difference between schools with supportive leaders and those with leaders who are both supportive and present. It is not uncommon to arrive at a school where teachers are being required to listen to me talk. Prior to arriving at the school, I make sure to remind the principal to be present for the meeting, to which he or she always agrees. It's easy to say you are going to be present, but principals are busy people, and the commitment made so easily over the phone is often just as easily forgotten. It's not unusual to have the principal introduce me to his or her teachers with an admonition to the teachers to pay careful attention to what I have to say. Of course, I appreciate the introduction, but I'm often dismayed as I watch the principal quickly exit the room. Presumably, this is because he or she has something much more important to do. While these principals appear to support their teachers, their departure from the room sends a much clearer message: it isn't important for me to be present.

Contrast those principals who are not present with the elementary school principal in Arizona who invited me to work with her teachers. Prior to beginning our training, the principal stood up and thanked the teachers for their hard work. She then asked the teachers to share some of the challenges they faced as they worked to implement the formative assessment process. Teachers responded openly by sharing their concerns about not having enough time in the day to get everything done. They shared their fears and frustrations. One teacher after another validated the previous teachers' concerns. It was rowdy, but I wouldn't call it complaining; it was an open, honest, and safe dialogue about real concerns and real frustrations.

The principal then shared with the teachers that she too had the same concerns based on the observations she had made while sitting in during their classes and team meetings. She shared her goals to help address the teachers' concerns and asked for their feedback. This was all happening right before I was scheduled to provide a full day of professional development. I began to wonder whether or not the teachers were going to be receptive to spending an entire day with me when that time could be used doing something else. The principal explained to the teachers why she had invited me to spend the day with them and why she felt it was important that everyone, including herself, was present.

Throughout our day together, she paused the discussion to make sure teachers understood and asked questions to help me better align my message to their needs. She made sure to give teachers time at the end to work together as teams and to ask individual questions. She sat down with each team and listened, offered suggestions, and laughed with her teachers. This principal was not just supportive of her teachers— she was present. She was present when they needed her to understand their challenges, and she was present as she helped to address many of those challenges. She had clearly gained the trust and support of her teachers through her actions and through her service.

School leaders often underestimate just how important their presence is to school morale. I am often struck by the unsolicited feedback I receive from teachers who share their feelings of being overwhelmed and unappreciated. Invariably they talk of feeling disconnected from their school leaders who are rarely present in their classrooms or team meetings. While I don't encourage or facilitate these conversations, I am always dismayed that the principal is not present to hear or address these teachers' concerns. Why? What could be more important than being present when your teachers need you the most?

When I talk to school leaders about the importance of being present, it is not unusual for principals to rattle off a list of challenges that, in their mind, make being present nearly impossible: teacher evaluations, student discipline, district meetings, district mandates, parent meetings, emergencies, faculty meetings, teacher issues, data management, test management, district report, and so on. While I empathize with these school leaders, I would ask one simple question: What matters most? The principal in Arizona certainly must deal with all of the above-mentioned challenges but somehow found the time to be present. She was present to hear her teachers' concerns and present to provide them support. The principal's enthusiasm for the work they were doing was infectious, and the teachers had clearly caught their principal's enthusiasm.

Being present matters! A principal who is present and supportive of the work being done in his or her school is creating the foundation that will lead to greatness. Each day will bring countless distractions that will challenge the most committed leader's ability to remain present and supportive of the important work being done in his or her school. Your school's success hinges on your ability to avoid, minimize, and manage those distractions. Your community, students, teachers, and staff need you. They need you to be present.

BALANCE OF MEASURES

Early in my career I think I spent far too much of my time focused on test scores.

Heartland Elementary School was built in 1982 in a suburb just south of Salt Lake City, Utah. The school was one of three K–6 elementary schools in the district utilizing an innovative modular construction method that would allow the school to be taken apart and relocated to another community if the population dwindled to a point at which the school was no longer needed. The school sat on piers three feet off the ground, with bouncy plywood floors and gravel-coated stucco exterior walls. There were six open classroom pods with one fully enclosed classroom designed to support four classes per grade level

(1–6) and one large pod assigned to two kindergarten classrooms. The only other enclosed classrooms were utilized for six high-needs, self-contained classrooms serving children with disabilities.

The surrounding neighborhood was made up of modest, middle-class, single-family homes and a large number of high-density multifamily housing units, mobile homes, and government-subsidized housing. The school received Title I funding and served a large number of students living in poverty. Nearly 30 percent of the students were learning English as a second language. With more than 700 students enrolled, student transiency was a constant and teacher turnover was common. Predictably, the school consistently scored in the bottom third of all schools in the state and was near the bottom of all schools in the large, mostly suburban school district.

Over a four-year period, I passed by Heartland Elementary School nearly every day on my way to work at a school just eight miles away. I often wondered what it would be like to work there. The school had not aged well. The gray stucco was dirty, and the simple box construction looked anything but welcoming. The grounds were void of all but a handful of trees, and the busy street out front often left me concerned about the safety of the students who needed to cross it every day. While I often wondered about the school, I had the luxury of passing it by as I continued on to my school—a school I assumed was much better.

In 1999 I was given the opportunity to serve as the principal of Peruvian Park Elementary. The school sat in the middle of a quiet, well-established neighborhood at the base of the Wasatch Mountains. The school was a classic, single-story, brick building built in 1962. Large windows stretched all the way across every classroom, letting in volumes of natural light. The building lacked air conditioning, the electrical system was lacking, and the school had seen very few upgrades over the years. This, however, didn't diminish the fact that the school just felt right when you walked through the front doors.

Every September, all fifty-five elementary school principals in the district would gather at the district office to receive the results of the previous year's end-of-level tests. We would all pick up a large manila envelope that contained our school's results. I wouldn't call it Christmas, but there was real excitement and anxiety in opening our long-awaited presents. I always looked forward to getting my school's results and never left disappointed. My school consistently scored in the top three schools in the district and was one of the highest scoring schools in the entire state. The opening of the manila envelope validated the hard work of the students and teachers in my school. It was a time to celebrate.

When the test scores of every school in the state were posted in the local newspaper, my phone would begin to ring. Parents from all over the valley would call in hopes of enrolling their children, and many would inquire about the real estate market in hopes of purchasing a house in our boundaries. Prospective teachers would call asking about potential teaching positions, and many of our own parents would call to congratulate us on our tremendous test scores. Only eight miles separated my school from Heartland Elementary, but it was clear from the end-of-level test results, the schools were clearly on two separate planets.

I loved analyzing our test results at Peruvian Park Elementary. I would pore over the data, looking for any areas of concern that we could target for improvement.

I would also call the principals in the surrounding schools to inquire about their results to see how we compared. Even though the data was gathered the previous year, the teachers and I would dutifully review the data together. Ultimately, we celebrated and took pride in the results that validated our hard work. In retrospect, while the results deservedly validated the hard work of the teachers, there were other factors that contributed to our rather predictable success.

During my time at Peruvian Park, we served 560 K–6 students. Our student population was extremely stable, with relatively few students moving in or out. The faculty was an outstanding mix of highly skilled, veteran teachers and a few dynamic, young teachers who, for the most part, got along well. We served fewer than ten students who were learning English as a second language and had a very modest number of students qualifying for free and reduced lunch. Peruvian Park also happened to be a magnet gifted and talented school. Over half the students in the school had tested and qualified for the accelerated learning program that provided instruction in math and language arts one full-graded level ahead.

Our test results afforded the teachers a tremendous amount of autonomy. Teachers were well respected in the community, and parents trusted that their child's needs were being met. There was plenty of time for the arts, innovation, and student projects. The school had many traditions of grade-level holiday performances, spelling bees, science fairs, and school plays. It was an inspiring place to work, and it provided me an incredibly safe place to begin my career as a school principal.

After four incredible years, I received a phone call from my boss informing me that I was being transferred to a new school. I had been anticipating a change and was excited to find out which school would become my new home. My new school was located just eight miles away, but when I found out I was headed to Heartland Elementary, I was certain I was going to that aforementioned new planet. All I knew of my new school was that it looked depressing from the outside and the test results were terrible. I was excited, scared, a little overwhelmed, and certain I was up for the challenge.

Perhaps the greatest mistake I made during my time at Heartland occurred within my first thirty seconds of finding out about my new assignment; it was to assume that the school's test scores and the quality of the school were somehow related.

When September rolled around, I found myself at the district office picking up the manila envelope for Heartland Elementary; No Child Left Behind was in its third year, and I was certain I was prepared for the inevitable. I pulled the papers from the envelope, scanned the results, and quickly realized my new school had failed to meet the AYP requirements. We had failed. Much to my surprise, I was mortified. A rush of emotions flooded me as I thought about the results inside the envelope belonging to my previous school. I knew they were good. I wanted to hold up those scores and declare them as my own. I had spent years at that school analyzing the results and had unknowingly allowed them to define me. I didn't want these failed results. *Failed*. That hurt.

As I returned to my new school, a school that felt surprisingly foreign to me, I was determined to do everything I could to ensure that next year's results would be different. I pored over the data, much like I had done in years past, and looked for areas of concern. It wasn't difficult. I emphasized the need to improve test scores throughout the school year. We focused specifically on math and language arts due to the fact that those were the two areas that would be tested. We focused on the Big Three elements of identifying student levels of readiness and understanding, targeting students for any needed intervention, and self-evaluating instructional practice. We held an assembly to motivate students to get a good night's sleep, eat a good breakfast, and most important, show up for the test.

I literally felt sick a year later as I held the envelope in my hands. I looked around at all of the other principals in the room and noticed I was not alone. The consequences of failure had increased over the last few years, and the thought of being labeled a failing school was terrifying, especially knowing that the results would be published in the paper for all to see. I felt a tremendous responsibility to my new community and to the teachers and staff in my school. A failing score would be embarrassing to everyone. With all of that in mind and after nearly every principal had already ended his or her suspense, I slowly pulled out the papers that felt toxic in my hands. The improvements were not dramatic, but we had somehow managed to pass.

I didn't feel like celebrating, and I didn't feel relieved. I was once again angry. Over the last year, I had come to realize one important fact: the test results, regardless of whether or not we passed, would never validate our hard work. I had come to realize that the teachers and staff at this school were some of the hardest working and most committed educators anywhere. I had grown to love the students, the parents, and the community more than I could have imagined. This was an amazing school. Students would arrive early in the morning for breakfast and were greeted by teachers who genuinely cared for them. Many of the students stayed for an after-school program that provided tutoring, mentoring, and a snack. These hollow test results left me with a new resolve to stop obsessing over test scores and start obsessing over doing everything we could to help every child to do better.

COUNTING THE WRONG THINGS

Why were Heartland's test scores so off the mark when it came to validating our hard work? Were we working harder but not smarter? Were there other factors involved? Heartland was a Title I school, and many studies have correlated socioeconomic status with student outcomes (HuffPost Politics, 2013). Studies have shown that specific factors around poverty can strengthen or weaken that correlation. For example, one reason poverty affects student outcomes is because it affects the amount of resources available to students (Lacour & Tissington, 2011). Another factor is the timing of poverty—how young a child is and for how long she lives in poverty. We were an elementary school, and poverty has a greater effect on student outcomes when young children are the ones living in it (Brooks-Gunn & Duncan, 1997). But perhaps poverty wasn't the only factor. Perhaps the tests themselves were not an accurate indicator of our hard work or our students' efforts.

The Rainbow Project (Sternberg & the Rainbow Project Collaborators, 2006) was a project based on different types of "successful intelligence," conducted by Robert J. Sternberg to see if the predictive value of the SAT test—a common requirement for college admissions—could be improved by testing three different types of intelligence (analytical, practical, and creative). Sternberg defines successful intelligence as "the ability to achieve success in life in terms of one's personal standards, within one's sociocultural context" (Sternberg & the Rainbow Project Collaborators, 2006). Analytical intelligence is the intelligence of school and, more specifically, of tests. It's the ability to analyze, evaluate, compare and contrast, and such. Practical intelligence is the ability to problem-solve—a sort of street smarts—or the ability to adapt to changes in your environment. Creative intelligence is the ability to create, invent, hypothesize, and such. Using these definitions of successful intelligence as a guide, we can surmise that students don't necessarily have to be superstars in all three in order to be successful in life.

What Sternberg found from his study was interesting as it applies both to tests and to children. Concerning tests, he found that multiple-choice questions measured analytical intelligence, regardless of what they were designed to measure (Sternberg, Bonney, Gabora, & Merrifield, 2012). This is important because it means that multiple-choice items—which even the new Smarter Balanced Assessment Consortium (SBAC) and Partnership for Assessment of Readiness for College and Careers (PARCC) exams use for half of their tests (Felton, 2015)—*only* measure analytical intelligence: the intelligence of tests.

Where students were concerned, Sternberg found that testing all *three* types of intelligence tended to reduce ethnic and racial group differences (Sternberg et al., 2012). In one of his studies, he found that while students in the high analytical group (i.e., the multiple-choice group) tended to be mostly white and middle class, students who scored well in the creative and practical groups were ethnically diverse; many students found themselves labeled "gifted" for the first time in their lives (Sternberg, 2009). He also found that combining the three types of intelligence could more accurately predict student success in college than using the SAT alone (Sternberg et al., 2012). So maybe these tests weren't capturing all of our students' learning. Maybe our hard work *was* smarter and not just harder.

The SBAC and PARCC tests are trying to balance the analytical portions of their tests with performance items, so theoretically they could be tapping into those other types of intelligences. This is good, but it neglects to address another problem, that of applying high-stakes accountability to these tests.

The problem with attaching high-stakes accountability to tests stems from the fact that people aren't particles. In the physical sciences, when scientists measure something under a certain set of conditions, they can reasonably assume that whatever they've measured—like a particle of dust, for example—will react the same way each time the conditions are met (Rothman, 1972). The particle doesn't *care* that it's being measured, so scientists can isolate variables and test different ones in order to test how the particle changes under different conditions, without worrying that the particle might change its behavior out of fear or greed or pride or any other uniquely *human* variable that could confound the test. But this doesn't work in the social sciences. Professor Donald T. Campbell noticed that when people are measured under high-stakes situations, they alter their behavior based on human characteristics. Specifically, "the more any quantitative social indicator is used for social decision-making, the more subject it will be to corruption pressures and the more apt it will be to distort and corrupt the social processes it is intended to monitor" (Campbell, 1976). This observation is known as "Campbell's Law" (Nichols & Berliner, 2005).

The Texas Miracle is an example of how this law works. The Texas Miracle refers to an approach to education implemented by Rod Paige in the Houston School District (Leung, 2004). Paige implemented a system of carrots and sticks for administrators. Principals who met district goals in areas like dropout rates and test scores got bonuses and other perks, while those who didn't were sanctioned, transferred, or forced out. At first glance, the district's results seemed amazing; "dropout rates plunged and test scores soared" (Leung, 2004). When history gave us a little perspective though, and investigators dug a little deeper, they found discrepancies in the results. Student dropout rates hadn't *plunged*; students were being falsely classified as transferring to another school or going home to a native country. Student outcomes hadn't *soared*; students who performed poorly in algebra and other subjects tested on the tenth-grade test were held back in ninth grade, then skipped ahead to eleventh grade. The high stakes attached to student outcomes and graduation rates were affecting principals' actions. Fear of losing a job or pursuit of gains in money or power tend to distort people's judgment that way. And students were losing out because of it.

The attachment of high-stakes accountability to tests encourages gross unethical behaviors like those found in the Texas Miracle, but it also affects education in more subtle ways. One example of more subtle effects of high-stakes accountability is the tendency to teach to the test. In a 1999 survey of North Carolina elementary teachers from five school districts across the state, "eighty percent of the teachers indicated that students [spent] more than 20% of their total instructional time practicing for the end-of-grade tests" (Jones, Jones, Hardin, Chapman, Yarbrough, & Davis, 1999, p. 201). This is distressing on two levels. Of course we don't want our children learning to take tests, but also, on a professional level, teachers are selling themselves short by focusing on test prep instead of focusing on the Big Three, focusing on improving their instructional practice in ways that can increase true student learning.

What's most ironic about high-stakes testing, though, is that it is doing the exact opposite of its original intent. High-stakes testing was meant to hold educators accountable for student learning. But what it's really doing is relieving educators of the responsibility of doing their jobs. Joseph Ganem, a physics professor and department chair at Loyola University Maryland, illustrated this point when he argued, "If the teachers are judged based on their students' test scores, there is no need to go into the classroom and observe their methods and interactions with students. Whether students are succeeding in spite of bad teaching or failing despite good teaching becomes irrelevant" (Ganem, 2011). Teachers don't have to own accountability when their evaluations are based on someone *else's* performance.

A TEST BY ANY OTHER NAME

NOUNS	ADJECTIVES
Assessment	Benchmark
Benchmark	Criterion-Based
Evaluation	Criterion-Referenced
Exam	Curriculum-Based
Judgment	Developmental
Measure	Diagnostic
Measurement	Formative
Observation	High-Stakes
Performance	Interim
Quiz	Norm
Task	Performance
Test	Readiness
	Standardized
	Summative

I created a quick list of words we use to describe that thing we do when we're trying to figure out something about learning. Each word has meaning, sometimes more than one. You've probably noticed that some words are in both columns. I'm sure I've missed some.

The two columns represent nouns and adjectives—nouns on the left, adjectives on the right (I didn't include verbs; I had to draw the line somewhere). When we look at articles, research, blogs, and social media, we see these words thrown around a lot. Sometimes the meanings get mixed up. Sometimes we find that one group uses one word one way, only to find that another group uses the same word a different way. For example, I've heard the word *benchmark* used as a summative benchmark, an interim benchmark, and a formative benchmark. It can also be standardized, performance-based, criterion-based, and, although I've yet to hear it described as such, norm-referenced. Sometimes the meanings get so jumbled that people have to clarify what they mean when they're referring to one of these names. This happens a lot in research articles. Here's a definition for "formative assessment":

> Formative assessment and its variations are the local, classroom version of formative evaluation (Scriven, 1967). Young and Kim (in press) point out that the term formative assessment is flexible, perhaps to the point of losing meaning. Those advocating *formative assessment* have used it to mean anything from informal or haphazard in-class judgment to frequent quantitative measures of specific skills. For the purposes of this article, *structured formative assessment* refers to the latter. (Dorn, 2010, p. 326)
>
> Oops. I forgot quantitative.

Formative and summative tend to have broad definitions that are generally understood. *Formative* means something used *during learning* usually to inform instruction and often not graded. *Summative* means something used *after learning* usually to provide a grade or some level of attainment. But if a teacher doesn't use a formative assessment to inform instruction, then is that assessment still formative? Or is it summative? If a teacher uses a test to inform instruction but also enters the scores in her gradebook, is that test formative or summative? Some of you may have definite definitions in your heads, and that's fine. But hopefully you can see the quandary around naming that thing we do when we're trying to figure out something about learning.

The point is that it doesn't really matter what we call that thing we do. What matters is what we use that thing *for*. So, for the purposes of the rest of this section, we'll call that we thing we do a "test."

Tests are just tests. It is we who assign meaning to them. Sometimes we associate a specific connotation with a specific test. For example, when I say "SAT" many of you may be thinking "college entrance exam" or "high-stakes test." It's possible that Sternberg had one of these connotations in mind when he did his Rainbow Project because in the findings of his report he indicated that:

> the analytical section of our test added little in terms of predictive power over and above the SAT. Because the SAT is already a well developed, reliable, and valid measure of

analytical skills, we plan to dispense with the analytical section in future versions of the Rainbow Project and simply use the SAT as our analytical measure. (Sternberg & the Rainbow Project Collaborators, 2006, p. 345)

The key idea we can infer from this quote is that the SAT can be used in more than one way. Sure, it's used as a high-stakes entrance exam that causes hopeful, future college students much grief and stress, but it can also be used in a different way. It can be used as a simple measure—not to inform a teacher's evaluation but simply to help determine what works and what doesn't. This sounds simplistic, but it is powerful. It is one of the Big Three—identify student levels of readiness and understanding.

When a test is used this way, it ceases to cause grief and stress. It ceases to encourage unethical practices. Instead it informs growth in the person using it. Not in the person *taking it*. Tests don't inform growth in of themselves. Not even formative ones. Tests just measure where a person is at that moment in time. But for the teacher using the test as a measure, it is a valuable clue into what works in his instruction.

The word *clue* is important here, too. Researchers often use a process called "triangulation." Triangulation makes me think of James Bond movies, when they're homing in on the bad guy using multiple tracking devices. Triangulation in research is essentially the same thing. It's homing in on an intervention—something new that's being tried—using multiple ways of collecting data. This is important because, as the Rainbow Project showed, there are also multiple definitions of *success*, *growth*, and *intelligence*. And no one test can measure them all. One of the biggest fallacies in society's attempt to enforce external accountability on schools and teachers was to try to do so using one, high-stakes test.

The point of all of this is that our current high-stakes tests don't necessarily need to go away. On the contrary, they can provide valuable clues into what's working in our instructional practice. But the "high-stakes" part does. As long as we are using tests to hold people hostage to their results in the name of accountability, we will find unethical practices and teaching to the test and corner-cutting and narrowing of the curriculum and all of the other distorted practices that come from our thirteen-year experiment with Campbell's law.

BALANCE OF PEOPLE

We began the following school year at Heartland with a completely new focus. We were very much aware that far too many of our students were reading well below grade level. I met with my first- and second-grade teams to discuss ways we could better meet the needs of our students. Our teachers had spent the last several years working to implement a balanced literacy approach and had struggled to fully implement the strategies in their classrooms. Each teacher was meeting with four or five differentiated, guided reading groups nearly every day. This meant that teachers were planning four or five separate small-group reading activities every single day as well as planning independent activities for the rest of the class while they worked with the small groups, and this was on top of their regular planning for the other subjects. The more we discussed the inherent challenges to implementing these strategies, the more we realized we had a one major obstacle to overcome: time.

Our solution was simple. It addressed the time issue as well as implemented the Big Three on a daily basis. Our student reading fluency and comprehension skills improved, and, depending on which teachers you asked, teacher preparation time went down. So what did we do?

We started with our first- and second-grade teams and began by working to determine an accurate reading level for every student. Students were leveled using the Fountas and Pinnell A–Z format. Our literacy facilitator either worked closely with each teacher or volunteered to assess each student to ensure consistency. Before placing the students in classes, the teachers ranked their top three choices for which class they would like to teach, and I then used that information to assign teachers. This allowed me to place teachers who were more comfortable teaching beginning readers in the lower groups, while those who were more comfortable teaching advanced readers were placed at the higher levels.

Each child was assigned to one of the eight first- and second-grade teachers for a ninety-minute reading block. This meant that classes consisted of both first- and second-grade students.

TEACHER	READING LEVELS	NUMBER OF STUDENTS
Teacher A w/aide	A	20-25
Teacher B w/aide	B-C	20-25
Teacher C	D-F	20-30
Teacher D	G-H	20-30
Teacher E	I-K	20-30
Teacher F	L-M	20-30
Teacher G	N-P	20-30
Teacher H	Q-Z	20-30

Without really knowing it, we were embarking on what would prove to be my first experience with a systematic implementation of mastery learning.

The term *mastery learning* was coined by the American educational psychologist Benjamin Bloom, more often known for the classification of learning objectives that he helped develop called "Bloom's Taxonomy" (Bloom, 1968). Mastery learning is an approach that attempts to individualize the pace of instruction to each student, progressing to more advanced learning topics only when earlier topics have been mastered. The easiest way to think about mastery learning is in the interplay between two key aspects of teaching: understanding and time. With traditional classroom instruction, time is held constant while understanding is allowed to fluctuate. Traditional teachers decide how much time to allocate to each topic—say, one unit chapter per week. The teacher covers that material in that amount of time, and it is up to the students to keep up. At the end of the week, the end-of-unit test shows who has understood the concepts and who hasn't, but either way, the class is moving on to the next unit.

Mastery learning attempts to flip that paradigm. Learning is held constant, and time is allowed to fluctuate. The ideal is that every student will learn the same amount but that some students will learn it faster and others will require more instruction. The approach has many critics because of the impracticability of individualizing instruction in overcrowded public classrooms, but it has been intriguingly employed in different settings over the years. Most notably, perhaps, by Carleton Washburne (1922) in the Winnetka, Illinois, school district in the 1920s, where students were individually promoted "on the basis of achievement rather than of time" (p. 195).

That was essentially what we were trying to implement at our school on the very limited curriculum of reading groups. But it was by no means an easy or risk-free enterprise. At the beginning, there was considerable concern that students would be embarrassed by their placement or that they would feel uncomfortable working with students a year older or a year younger. We were concerned that we would end up creating a system that simply ability-grouped students and kept them from actually moving up. We were also very concerned that parents would share those concerns. Additionally, we were concerned with how much time it would take to reassess every student every three weeks. We crafted a letter to the parents that explained our plan and solicited their feedback.

I credit the incredible trust the teachers had established over the years with the community to the fact that we didn't receive a single phone call. I was also careful to distribute the teachers throughout the reading levels so that students wouldn't automatically assume that a second-grade teacher indicated higher reading levels and a first-grade teacher indicated lower reading levels. The teachers were very cognizant of the concerns, and after a few weeks of planning, we were ready to begin.

Our teachers were meeting in small groups with every student on a daily basis, identifying student levels of understanding through formative assessments, targeting students for interventions, and self-evaluating instructional practice. We had initially planned to assess all the students every other week to facilitate moving students from group to group as they progressed. This never really happened, though, as teachers began to communicate directly with each other on an ad hoc basis about individual student needs. Teacher A might talk to Teacher B to let her know that she had a student who was ready to move up. This would result in a conversation with teachers C and D to evaluate their needs. Students would move from teacher to teacher as needed, and the reading levels being taught evolved to match the changing dynamics of the group. It is also worth noting that we were able to place teacher assistants in our two lowest reading groups and managed to minimize class sizes at those levels. We also engaged our special education team and worked to provide these additional services within the context of the reading block itself. This was a decision made by the teachers and one that allowed us to provide additional supports to our most at-risk students.

The concerns we had about mixing grade levels were unfounded. What we found was that the students began to thrive in an environment where the teachers were completely focused on their specific needs. Teachers also found that they were able to spend their time preparing better instruction due to the fact that they were now able to focus on a much narrower band of reading levels.

We tracked individual progress on a large magnetic whiteboard. Each grade level's magnets were painted a different color, and each student was assigned a number. At the beginning of the year, we placed the magnets on the board based on a student's reading level with a matching sticker underneath. As students moved from one level to another, their magnet was moved to mark their progress. The sticker remained at the original starting point so that we could track growth. Teachers would provide updates to the literacy facilitator, who would move the magnets. The board became a visual representation of our progress. We could quickly identify students who were struggling to make progress and work to provide appropriate interventions.

At a certain point, I began to get requests from teachers asking to switch reading groups. Shuffling teachers created some unexpected but positive outcomes. As teachers transitioned to their new reading groups, they began to question the methods used to level the students. Teachers noticed that the levels assigned by the previous teacher were not in alignment with their evaluations. One teacher might identify a student as a level M, while another would level that same student at a level P. This created opportunities for the teachers to collaborate and discuss ways to improve their practice. We met as a team with the literacy facilitator to address the discrepancies and worked together to create solutions and share ideas. These conversations served to create greater consistency in how students were being evaluated and served. The change also created opportunities for teachers to collaborate. A teacher who was assigned a new reading group would often seek out the previous teacher to gain insight into what had been done previously and discuss ways to expand and improve her practice.

Throughout the school year, we began to see impressive results across both grade levels. But I believe the greatest and most unexpected outcomes were those dealing with relationships with students. We ended up shuffling teachers three or four times a year. The movement of teachers combined with the movement of students virtually guaranteed that, over a two-year period, a student would eventually receive reading instruction from every first- and second-grade teacher. This meant that every teacher knew every student. When a teacher ran into students in the hallway or on the playground, he or she could address them by name. There were no anonymous students. Because the students were assigned to teachers and not grade levels, students developed friendships with peers in both grade levels. We expanded the reading program the following year to include third and fourth grades as well as fifth and sixth grades. The results were consistent across all grade levels. This meant that each year our starting levels were slightly higher than the previous year, and most important, I could honestly tell every parent who had a child in my school that we were providing daily targeted instruction that met the specific needs of their child regardless of reading levels.

The question remained, however, what the overall impact of all these efforts would be. We knew we were making a difference in the lives of our readers, but would these individual differences roll up, so to speak, into higher end-of-level assessment scores? Would they show up in the state data and help us achieve AYP? As the end of the year approached, we braced ourselves for the scores.

THE EXPERT PROBLEM

I had been true to my commitment. We had focused on the plan, not the test scores. We knew we were making a difference in the lives of our readers. So why were we bracing ourselves? Why were we listening to someone potentially thousands of miles away? Someone who didn't know us. Someone who didn't know our students.

One reason may have to do with the way society currently perceives expertise. Theodore M. Porter (n.d.), a history professor at the University of California at Los Angeles, studies and teaches the history of science, emphasizing "science did not always idealize this mechanical form of objectivity [i.e., quantification], but has come to do so (at least in its rhetoric) as an adaptation to modern political and administrative cultures—which it at the same time has helped to shape." Society trusts numbers, not opinions.

Douglas Carnine (2000), a professor of education at the University of Oregon, used Porter's idea—that mature professions tend to place more value on standardized measures than on personal trust—to support his argument that education is an immature profession not to be entirely trusted. This inherent lack of trust in education's experts, combined with a societal emphasis on quantification, greatly influenced the NCLB reauthorization of ESEA, which includes requirements for scientifically based research and even includes its own (very wordy) definition of the term (United States of America 107th Congress, 2002).

Porter urged education to model its transformation to a mature profession after medicine's example. The field of medicine had taken over a century to evolve from individual expert opinions to quantitative measures and had been forced by external pressures to do so (Carnine, 2000). Porter highlights the Food and Drug Administration (FDA) as an example. The FDA initially accepted opinions as well as study results when deciding whether to approve a drug. This worked until the thalidomide tragedy in the early 1960s, during which the drug thalidomide caused birth defects in hundreds of children whose mothers had used it for morning sickness. After that, drugs had to be proven effective before they could be used, and medicine became firmly planted in the quantitative camp (Carnine, 2000).

The use of medicine as an example is an interesting choice. At first glance, there certainly seem to be some things in common. For example, medicine used to rely on tradition, personal experience, and subjective opinions. Education often does the same today. But there are a few other factors we need to consider when making this comparison.

Porter's comparison is based on the assumption that medicine's use of scientifically based research is valid and reliable. But John Ioannidis, a professor of Health Research and Policy at the Stanford School of Medicine, blew that assumption out of the water. His studies show that between 10 and 80 percent of medical studies, depending on the type of study, are flat-out wrong and that "at every step in the process, there is room to distort results, a way to make a stronger claim or to select what is going to be concluded....There is an intellectual conflict of interest that pressures researchers to find whatever it is that is most likely to get them funded" (Freedman, 2010). Medical science's "superior" method is not immune to Campbell's Law either.

My earlier observation that people aren't particles is another factor to consider. James Shanteau (1992), a psychologist and professor at Kansas State University, identified five factors that influence expertise: (1) domain knowledge, (2) psychological traits, (3) cognitive skills, (4) the use of decision strategies, and (5) task characteristics. The fifth one, task characteristics, sheds additional light as to why this comparison isn't quite apples to apples. Shanteau organizes task characteristics into two columns—one that experts usually perform well on, and the other where they tend to perform poorly. The good performance tasks tend to be static, predictable, and objective—tasks that medical researchers often do. The poor performance tasks tend to be changing, unpredictable, and subjective (Shanteau, 1992). The "series of complex human events" that make up teaching and learning are among these poor performance tasks. One of the more interesting findings Shanteau refers to is the fact that society expects different levels of expertise based on these tasks. We would think that experts doing good performance tasks would be held to a higher standard of accountability than those doing poor performance tasks, but the exact opposite is true! We expect *more* from people like expert teachers than we do from people like expert physicians (Shanteau, 1992).

One last observation: Let's say for a moment that quantitative research *is* the best type of research, and that medicine *does* compare apples to apples with education. There is still one more thing to consider. Both medicine and education have been or are being pressured from the outside to increase the validity of their professions, but medicine transformed from the *inside*. It increased its *own* standards and owned its accountability. The scientific community goes ballistic over any outside interference with its standards of accountability (Freedman, 2010).

Why don't we?

BE THE EXPERT YOU WANT TO SEE
IN THE WORLD

What I learned at Heartland Elementary completely changed my belief that high-stakes test scores are an effective measure of a school's success and the students', teachers', and staff's hard work. Never in my career—including during my time at a magnet school with exceptionally high test scores—had I worked harder or with teachers who were more dedicated.

We had begun our plan in hopes of better meeting the needs of all of our students. We hoped this would translate into better results on the end-of-level assessments but never let that outweigh our original goal. We knew we needed to address the challenges of time. The teachers were the problem solvers, they were the drivers of the process, and they were ultimately responsible for making it work. A school that functions as a committed team is key to finding solutions. We believed that if we faithfully implemented the Big Three and focused on meeting the immediate needs of students, the end-of-level tests would reflect the increased levels of learning our students had experienced.

Ultimately, we felt that the results were disappointing. We shifted our end-of-level percentile but never by enough to satisfy the district leadership or, indeed, to attract any public attention to what we were doing. We did not see the kind of turnaround that we had hoped for because we were looking to the wrong people. We were expecting the experts—people far away and unknown to us or to our situation—to validate our hard work, without realizing that *we* were the experts. *We* were the ones who had the expertise to speak to our students' growth. We were the ones who could share the results of our hard work with our parents and our supervisors and our community. We missed an opportunity to reclaim our school and classrooms because we didn't understand the true nature of expertise. Let's break it down by Shanteau's (1992) five factors to see what could have led us to miss this opportunity.

① **Domain Knowledge:** Domain knowledge isn't just book smarts; it's also street smarts, "the insights gained from experience in working on real problems" (Shanteau, 1992). We may or may not have had the same level of textbook knowledge of those who created the test, but we certainly had the real-world experience.

(2) **Psychological Traits:** Psychological traits include self-confidence, communication, the ability to adapt, a sense of responsibility—basically we needed to *act* like experts. Here we only partially succeeded. We definitely felt a sense of responsibility, and we were able to adapt internally, but we weren't confident in our ability to communicate what we found *externally*. We were afraid.

(3) **Cognitive Skills:** Cognitive skills include the ability to maintain focus and a sense of what's relevant under stress. We certainly had *that*! It's also the ability to identify exceptions to rules. In this, our fear of external accountability overshadowed our ability to break the rules that had been placed on education about who's the expert.

(4) **Decision Strategies:** Experts use strategies such as making use of feedback, finding and using things to help with decision making, breaking down complex problems, and pre-thinking solutions. We did all these things when preparing and implementing our plan.

(5) **Task Characteristics:** Our task—to help students become better readers—was a complex, dynamic, subjective task, as illustrated by our collaboration

around different evaluations of student reading levels. This is not something we could change. But we *did* do things to help provide more structure, such as using our magnetic whiteboard and communicating regularly with each other.

We overwhelmingly met the conditions of expertise as defined by Shanteau—except in one area. We didn't act like experts. Our fear of external accountability kept us from communicating our results in a way that would also communicate our expertise. And even if we had, the atmosphere at the time may have dampened our ability to fully own our accountability. But it took the medical community 100 years to own theirs—we have to start somewhere.

BALANCE OF MARKET-BASED REFORM

Like nearly every kid in my neighborhood, I grew up playing a variety of sports and activities. We would gather in backyards or playgrounds, choose up sides, and play baseball, football, and basketball late into the night. We would organize for games of kick-the-can, freeze tag, street tennis, and all manner of made-up games. We would gather in my best friend's basement, strap on the boxing gloves, and pummel each other. Participating in sports was a way to bring all of us together. It was an essential part of building our own community and provided all of us with a sense of belonging. I loved the competition, but I cherished most the friendships that made those activities possible.

As I became more involved in organized sports, the competition became more intense and the perceived stakes increased accordingly. Throughout my child-hood, I was hypercompetitive. This was a trait that proved to be both a blessing and a curse. I was moti-vated by the competition, but I didn't always display the best sportsmanship. I was known to have thrown my bat after striking out or being less than gracious after a loss. It took me a long time to learn the merits of sportsmanship—how to win respectfully and lose gra-ciously. It is often cliché to compare sports to life, but for me the comparison is apropos.

It was sport that taught me the value of collaboration, determination, and the value of doing your best. It was sport that allowed me to see that life isn't always fair—you win some and you lose some. It was sport that taught me to appreciate and root for the incredible in others—you are not always going to be the best, but you can always appreciate the best in others. It was sport that provided insight into the value of knowing the difference between competition and collaboration, and that there is a time for both.

MARKET PRINCIPLES: COMPETITION AND PUBLIC SCHOOLS

Our market economy mirrors sports in many ways. It too is a combination of collaboration and competition, although when we think of a market economy we tend to focus on the competitive element.

A market economy is "a capitalistic economic system in which there is free competition and prices are determined by the interaction of supply and demand" (Market Economy, n.d.). The United States is based on a market economy, and although the public's perceptions of the word *capitalism* are mixed (50 percent positive, 40 percent negative), there is a general acceptance of our current system, especially in comparison to other systems such as socialism (Pew Research Center, 2011). We understand that there are some downsides to a market economy—greed, inequality, unequal opportunities—but we accept these because we also know that a market economy encourages wealth, opportunity for all, personal responsibility, and individual freedom (Jones, Cox, Navarro-Rivera, Dionne, & Galston, 2013).

Historically, schools have operated largely *outside* of the market economy. Traditionally, one of the primary roles of schools was to "form national citizens who are politically loyal, uphold the *status quo*, support the State in times of crisis, and help to sustain narratives that are essential for preserving the integrity of the State" (Desjardins, 2015, p. 1). This underlying philoso-phy of education, as well as education's compulsory nature and public source of funding, kept it clear of market forces, categorizing it instead as a public good, not unlike police services and libraries.

After *A Nation at Risk* brought into question the quality of our public schools, the market-based phi-losophies around education that had been bubbling just under the surface for years began to rise. Pro-ponents of market-based education reform believe that implementing a supply-and-demand structure so that parents can exercise freedom of choice will save taxpayers money, boost student test scores, help chil-dren rise from poverty, and weaken the teacher unions that they view as barriers to reform (FreedomWorks,

2011). In 1994, politicians on both sides of the aisle agreed that the idea of school choice was a good one, so they included the ability to create public charter schools, as well as increased flexibility for school choice within traditional public schools, in the Clinton administration's reauthorization of the Elementary and Secondary Education Act. Public vouchers have also been approved in limited cases at the state level (for example, those found in Milwaukee, Washington DC, and New York) (Ladd, 2002).

Another area that market-based reform focuses on is that of teacher merit pay. *A Nation at Risk* recommended that we make teaching a more rewarding and respected profession. Advocates of merit pay believe it will do just that. Teachers have long advanced according to a steps-and-ladders approach that combines years of experience with levels of education. This approach minimizes competition and rewards experience and knowledge. Advocates of merit pay believe that merit pay has the potential to incentivize teachers to work harder and produce better results, make the teaching profession look more attractive to bright, new recruits and help to address the problem of low teacher salaries (Lewis, n.d.). Different approaches to merit pay have been consistently explored in districts through-out the country since the 1980s (Morrison, 2013).

These market-based reforms have had varying levels of successful implementation within our public system. School choice has been implemented most success-fully, with more than 6,000 public charter schools in operation at the beginning of the 2012–2013 school year (Hechinger Report, 2014). You may have noticed though that I was careful to tie these market-based reforms with their successful *implementation*, not their *overall* success. The research around the success of market-based reforms for key indicators such as stu-dent outcomes, costs, innovation, teacher performance, and so on is mixed. There are occasionally studies that highlight charter schools or vouchers or merit pay as wildly successful, but they are in the minority, and their results have been at times questioned due to method-ology, sampling, or other reasons (Ladd, 2002). I could go into a lengthy discussion of the evidence behind the statement I just made, but will instead let you gather and explore that evidence for yourself because it is not my intent to bash market-based reforms. I prefer instead to explore a few reasons why these reforms may sometimes struggle and to propose looking at reform in education from a different point of view.

The market economy seems to work just fine in a lot of areas, so why does it seem to struggle in the area of education? A clue to one reason it may struggle can be found in the definition of "public good." A public good tends to exhibit two characteristics: (1) it's not competitive—if I check out a book from the library it doesn't mean there are fewer books for everyone else because I'm going to bring it back; and (2) it's inclusive—if I protect a community, everyone in that community benefits (EconomicsHelp.org, n.d.). Public education is inclusive—every child has the right (is required, actually) to attend school. No one's left out. Until recently, it also wasn't competitive. Where you lived determined where you went to school. We've always had private schools, of course, but there aren't enough of them (and they cost too much) to provide true competition.

When advocates of market-based reform began introducing competition in the area of school choice, there was a problem, however. A market economy relies on the ability for poorly performing businesses to *fail*, meaning they go out of business. But how does a poorly performing school *fail*? Where do its students go? Does the district bus them somewhere else? Does it replace the closed school with a new one? Does a charter school step in to take its place? Perhaps the compulsory nature of schools—the fact that the same students who went to the failed school now go to the charter school that replaced it—contributes to research that shows that charter schools tend to have no better or worse student test scores than comparable public schools (Di Carlo, 2011).

Another principle that a market economy employs is the ability to control its raw goods. Whether the goods are blueberries or people doesn't really matter. What matters is that businesses can get rid of them if they're not up to par. But how does a school get rid of its raw goods? How does it fire its students if they're performing poorly? It can't. Traditional public schools can't pick and choose their students (apart from special programs such as gifted and talented). They must take them all. This tends to make for unfair competition; only in this case, the competition tends to *favor* charter schools instead of work against them because charter schools benefit from a soft positive bias—parents who have the desire and means to get their children there.

Public schools, especially those serving traditionally poor-performing students, suffer because they lose resources as they lose students (Ladd, 2002).

Some may argue that these poor performing schools should innovate—find ways to attract new students. But this is a simplistic response that doesn't take into account the third factor affecting school choice: the fact that parents have *already* been choosing schools for years. Earlier, in my story about my time at Peruvian Park, I mentioned that parents would call to find out about the real estate market within my school boundaries. For decades, parents have been choosing schools based on where they choose to live. Ladd illustrated that "parents [tend to] judge a school's quality in part by the socioeconomic composition of its student body" (Ladd, 2002, p. viii). This makes the playing field inherently not level. It also makes it difficult for a poor high-needs school that's losing students to market-based school choice to attract students from high-income households.

Advocates of market-based reform believe that infusing competition into education will make it better, but businesses in the free market are beginning to realize something that education has known all along. Although competition is great *between* companies—it fosters innovation and efficiency—competition isn't so great *within* a company. Within a company it's imperative that employees trust each other and work together. Collaboration is key. "Two minds are better than one" and "Many hands make light work" didn't become old adages because they're linguistically exquisite, but because they're right.

One of the most famous examples of intra-company collaboration is that of Toyota's transformation to lean. The concept of "lean" originates in a process that Toyota created in the '50s in order to reduce waste and increase quality in its automotive factories (Ohno, 1988). In this process, waste is the bad guy. Perfection is the goal. But knowing that perfection is an impossible goal to reach, a continuous dedication to excellence takes its place. Think of perfection like this: If we try to divide the number 1 in half, and then in half again, and then in half again, and so on, trying to divide our way to zero, we will never reach it. We can always divide by another 2. (If you try this on a calculator you may get an endless 0.00000000000001 or strange number/letter combinations like 9.537E-7, but if you get a zero your calculator is giving up.) This example illustrates the concept of uncountable infinity. It's not the *destination* that's important because it's impossible to arrive there. It's the *journey* that matters. This is the first of Toyota's two top-level objectives: the focus on continuous improvement, what I'll call continuous learning (Ohno, 1988).

To understand Toyota's second top-level objective, let's return to Toyota's original process. A key component of Toyota's lean management approach was giving workers autonomy to stop the line. Imagine the factory line in *Charlie and the Chocolate Factory*—an endless pile of toothpaste caps that must be fitted *just right* to an endless line of toothpaste tubes (Burton, 2005). Under American factory processes, if a cap was faulty in some way, it was still fitted to the toothpaste tube. Then, at the end of the line, the entire assembled item was removed, set aside, and fixed (often not well, sometimes not at all). The goal was quantity, so the line could *never ever* stop. Even if workers knew something was wrong, they were not allowed to stop the line to fix it. Toyota turned this logic on its head when it gave its workers autonomy to stop the assembly line. Workers were empowered to make decisions that would *temporarily* delay the process, but *overall* increase quality. This autonomy worked because of Toyota's second top-level objective: the focus on respect for others (Ohno, 1988).

Toyota took this process to America in 1984 when it partnered with GM to reopen a previously closed plant as the NUMMI plant in California (Glass, 2010). A never-stop-the-line expectation had been firmly rooted in the culture of the previous plant. Managers didn't trust workers to make autonomous decisions, and workers didn't trust managers to help them. As part of the reopening, rehired managers and workers went through an intense training program to learn the new lean management system. American workers were nervous but also excited to apply this new system of autonomy and accountability, symbolized by their ability to stop the line.

Continuous learning and mutual respect won the day, and the NUMMI plant experienced great success. And since the early '80s, variations of Toyota's lean management style have expanded far beyond the automobile industry. It now reaches into technology, business, healthcare, and more. Businesses and services alike are beginning to benefit from principles *already* understood by education that emphasize trust and collaboration, *not* competition.

It's easy to understand why applying market-based reforms to education appeals to so many people outside of education. We are a country that loves competition and expects to be the very best at everything we do. We expect to win the most gold medals at the Olympics. We expect our companies to be the most innovative and lucrative. We expect and understand that there will be winners and losers in a market-based system. But the desire to create a school system that rewards winners and penalizes losers is in direct conflict with the very foundational underpinnings of that system—public schools exist for the good of the public.

We as a society owe each child, regardless of gender, ethnicity, race, or socioeconomic status, access to a free public education. An education that is free from the market forces that create inequality through a system that requires that some will win and some will lose. An education that provides access to equitable opportunities for all students regardless of circumstance. Public education understands this. It understands that in order to provide these equitable opportunities, education cannot be in competition with *itself*, because when it is, the real losers are the students we cannot fire, those we cannot get rid of, the students who need us the most. The solutions to improving our schools will most likely not be found outside of our current system, they will be found from within.

AUTONOMY, MASTERY, AND PURPOSE

Some of you may be wondering why I have included any references to business in a book about education. A few years ago, I left the public school system to join an educational technology (ed-tech) start-up I helped co-found with a few friends. It wasn't something I had planned; it just happened. We developed a software platform engineered to help teachers in my school better implement the elements of the Big Three. Over the course of several years, teachers, schools, and districts all over the country began to adopt our software. Two years into the project, I was confronted with a difficult decision: continue to watch the company grow from afar, or leave public education and join our start-up full time. The transition into the business world was surprisingly difficult. I was a bit like a fish out of water. Over the course of the last several years, I have come to realize the inherent similarities and differences that exist between the public and private sectors.

One of these differences is a tendency for businesses to emphasize externally motivated rewards and punishments in an effort to influence behavior (for example, raises and promotions versus firings). But just as businesses are beginning to realize the inherent worth of collaboration within a company, they are also beginning to realize that when dealing with complex tasks the traditional carrots-and-sticks approach to business doesn't work so well either, just as it doesn't work so well for the "series of complex human events" found in education.

Author Daniel Pink (2009) shares some insight about this during his TED Talk, "The Puzzle of Motivation":

> These contingent motivators—if you do this, then you get that—work in some circumstances. But for a lot of tasks, they actually either don't work or, often, they do harm. This is one of the most robust findings in social science, and also one of the most ignored.

Pink (2011) introduces three elements of intrinsically motivated behavior—autonomy, mastery, and purpose—and identifies them as elements that are necessary for businesses that involve complex processes. Education, which also involves complex processes, understood and embraced these behaviors before the swing toward external accountability, recognizing their importance in helping teachers gain mastery of their instructional practice as they gained experience in their profession. Let's take a closer look at these three factors as they relate to teaching and learning using the example of competency-based learning.

Competency-based learning (also called competency-based education) is the ability for students to learn in a more personalized manner, where they can advance based on their mastery of concepts rather than on traditional seat time (U.S. Department of Education, n.d.). Competency-based learning can help meet students' individual learning needs, but it's based on the assumption that students have the qualities of autonomy and mastery, and to a lesser extent, purpose. Students, however, aren't *born* with high levels of these qualities (except for outliers, of course); they must learn them. One of the most powerful ways to learn new behaviors is through modeling (Bandura, 1977)—through watching others behave that way—and one of the best opportunities for watching others that students have is in the classroom. It's an excellent opportunity for them to learn autonomy, mastery, and purpose, but only if their teachers are modeling these qualities.

AUTONOMY

Autonomy is the ability to self-direct, to work hard without external control or influence. Pink (2009) argues that carrot-and-stick methods of management work well when you seek compliance, but not when you seek engagement. If engagement is your goal, then you need to provide autonomy. Teachers with autonomy don't just follow a prescribed lesson or curriculum guide or textbook, they adjust it to meet the needs of their students or ignore it if it doesn't include the information they need. They modify lesson plans to address student realizations they may not have anticipated. They model hard work when opportunities might arise for a little slacking off. Students see this; they see the autonomous decisions. They see the deviations from the planned (and sometimes prescribed) lessons. They understand the difference between a teacher they can get off task and one who keeps them on *task while addressing unplanned questions. They learn the value of autonomy from teachers who are autonomous.*

MASTERY

Pink (2009) describes mastery as "the desire to get better and better at something that matters." We talk about student mastery of this and student mastery of that, and that's good. But we don't talk much about a student's *desire* to get better as being part of mastery. Being a lifelong learner isn't the same as learning. Students need to learn how to *want* to learn. And you guessed it, seeing that in action is a powerful way to begin learning mastery. Teachers with mastery try new things in the classroom. They admit they don't know it all and search out answers, and they encourage students to do the same. They continuously improve their professional skills in order to gain mastery of their profession. Students see this. They see a teacher who has mastery, as defined by Pink, in the way she teaches and listens and interacts. Students pick up on teachers' enthusiasm, on their insatiable desire to continuously find better ways of ensuring learning.

PURPOSE

Pink (2009) describes purpose as a "yearning to do what we do in the service of something larger than ourselves." This idea of purpose was always central to the answer of every person I ever hired to work in my school. Teaching without purpose isn't teaching. Teachers with purpose improve their instructional practice because they want to better help their students and more confidently communicate with their communities. They connect their students' learning with issues facing our society. They encourage reflection and problem solving around these issues. When students see this, they begin to understand that there is more to life than the next new gadget. They begin to increase their circles of empathy and of influence.

Advocates of market-based reform have worked hard to introduce competitive market principles into education, assuming that these principles will make it better, just as it makes businesses better. But maybe, just maybe, the competitive principles aren't the most effective ones to introduce. Students watch teachers every day. They see teachers at their best and at their worst. They act as teachers act. If students are to learn the skills they need to succeed not just in school, but in life in general, and if teachers are to successfully own their accountability and reclaim their classrooms, then teachers need a return to the ability to collaborate—not compete—with their colleagues, and they need respect from their peers and superiors. Teachers need the return of autonomy, mastery, and purpose so that they can effectively implement the Big Three. It's these internal collaborative principles that teachers need if we're to find and implement solutions to improving our schools from within.

CHAPTER 3
LAYING A CLAIM TO ACCOUNTABILITY

STACY WAS A SIXTH-GRADE STUDENT IN MY ELEMENTARY SCHOOL. She was bright, bilingual, and packed with energy. She, and around twenty-five of her fifth- and sixth-grade classmates, had been identified as students who were reading significantly below grade level. I met with Kris, my reading coach, to brainstorm ways to accelerate the reading progress of these students. Kris had taught first grade for over twenty years and was an expert in teaching students to read. She agreed to team-teach Stacy's class and implement the Big Three to provide targeted daily interventions for every student in the class in the most effective way possible.

For whatever reason, Kris and Stacy hit it off. Stacy began to improve almost immediately. She asked for additional tutoring and for books to take home. She quickly moved from that class to the next level and soon after to the next. Stacy had set a goal to become one of the top readers in the sixth grade by the end of the year and was nearly there with only a few weeks left before dismissal.

Each day, she would return to school with tales of a new book she was reading, and with each day, her fluency and comprehension improved. She was fearless and committed to doing whatever she needed to do to reach her goal. She had found a friend and a champion in Kris, who worked tirelessly to help all of the students make progress but who took a personal interest in helping Stacy achieve her seemingly impossible goal. It was the final week of school, or very near that, when Stacy was moved into the highest reading class in the school. Those of us who watched Stacy's progress throughout the school year were inspired by her courage and her tenacity. She had made greater progress in a single year than any student in the entire school. There were tears of joy streaming down their faces as Stacy and Kris entered my office to share the news of Stacy's triumph. For those who ever doubted Stacy, and I am sure there were times when she doubted herself, she had proven them wrong. For anyone who questioned whether or not a student could make a four- or five-year gain in reading comprehension and fluency in a single year, Stacy had settled it. It was possible.

The mythology of "Stacy" found circulating through the boardrooms, halls, and classrooms in American schools is as powerful to many educators as the myths of Zeus and Apollo were to the Greeks. For many educators, hope comes from the belief that the work they have committed themselves to will someday produce a bountiful harvest equal to those they have seen in movies and read about in books.

Educators are moved by the heroic efforts of teachers in *Mr. Holland's Opus, Stand and Deliver, Freedom Writers*, and *Dangerous Minds*. Book after book outlines the steps required to entreat the education gods to gather the clouds and bless the arid school grounds with rains of knowledge. For many teachers, the idea that miracles are possible, and that somehow, somewhere out there, another teacher just like them has found the teaching Holy Grail, gives them hope to continue moving forward.

Unfortunately, the rains the gods bring are most often tears of frustration and disappointment. While most of us accepted early on that teaching would be difficult, the vast majority of us enter our classrooms unprepared for the crushing weight of reality. Those books and movies that may have inspired our desire to teach or sustained us as we worked our way through college end up serving as barometers of our failure to meet our own unrealistic expectations. The sound of our own opus fades as the hopes of students standing on their desks, looking straight into our eyes, and passionately quoting from Old Walt himself, "Oh Captain, my Captain" (Weir, 1989) turn to inward thoughts of, "Oh hell, my hell, what am I going to do now?"

But, it's being done elsewhere, right? By someone else. We begin to question why *we* are unable to summon the storm clouds when we have heard of schools and classrooms in far-off places where the rains of knowledge give way to a lush Eden of learning. Much like the idyllic hamlet of Lake Wobegon, there are supposedly places where all of the women are strong, all of the men are good looking, and all of the children are above average. "Why then am I not feeling strong or particularly good looking, and why, despite all of my efforts, are only some students, only a few, above average? Why am I unable to do what others have done? What are they doing that I am not?" The questions lead one to seek answers from the books and experts who have been there and done that. They lead us on a quest to find the Holy Grail using the cryptic maps they provide, and after much searching, much trial and error, most of us find ourselves right back where we began.

Stacy's story reinforces the myth that society has placed upon us, and society holds us accountable for *every* student as if she were a Stacy. But Stacy is an outlier. Stacy had that rare combination of natural curiosity and determination that drove her to incredible levels of achievement. We focus on Stacy in the story and fail to recognize all the non-Stacys, just as we don't see the gorilla in that Invisible Gorilla video (Simons,

2010). We are so focused on the outlier that we forget there were twenty-five other students who received the same attention that Stacy did. Why didn't they show the same improvement as Stacy? Is it because Kris wasn't an effective teacher? (She was.) Should I have included that discrepancy among students on her evaluation? (Absolutely not!)

The Big Three distills into a simple representation the complex system of teaching and learning. A balance of all three elements combined with trust in those tasked with implementing them is required in order for this complex system to work. Over the course of the last thirty years, forces in our society have slowly eroded the trust the public once had in our schools and in our teachers and replaced it with external, high-stakes accountability based on only one part of one element of the Big Three: a test score. But judging our effectiveness using unrealistic criteria, misplaced measures, and unqualified evaluators is not true accountability. Public education is a complex organization working to address complex problems. The pathway to regaining the public trust and restoring balance of the Big Three will invariably take time and be complex. But there are three things we can implement right now to begin restoring this trust and balance.

1. We can own the results of all elements of the Big Three.
2. We can own conversations around true accountability.
3. We can own the noise.

OWNING THE RESULTS OF THE BIG THREE

I was fourteen years old when I first walked into my junior high metals shop. I came from a home where the sum of our tools consisted of a hammer, screwdriver, and a pair of pliers, so nearly every tool and device in the shop was new to me. School was the only opportunity I was going to have to learn to work with my hands, and I was motivated to make the most of it. I can remember the agony of the first few weeks of class, as we spent nearly every minute learning about the wide variety of tools we were going to use, shop safety, and the basic math and measurement skills we were expected to master before we could enter the shop. Once we completed our orientation, we were subjected to a rigorous exam that, once passed, signaled our readiness to begin bending, shaping, and welding metal. I didn't fear the test, as it consisted of demonstrating a perfect understanding of the things we had discussed in class. The test seemed reasonable and necessary.

I can remember the distinct smell of oil and metal that greeted me each time I walked into the classroom: a smell that signaled a respite from the part of my school day that had me sitting in a desk solving math problems, diagramming sentences, and searching for the answers at the back of the chapter while reading my history or science text. While I excelled in my math, English, social studies, and science classes, I didn't enjoy them. I didn't look forward to any of them, and I rarely felt inspired while sitting dutifully through them. This isn't a knock on my teachers, rather a reflection of where my personal interests were at the time. Drama, music, PE, and shop were a different story—I rushed to those classes and relished the opportunity to move, to create, and to engage in learning with my hands.

I can remember learning to use the spot-welder, the metal brake, the large sheet-metal press, aviation snips, the assorted files, drills, and tap and dies. I made an eyebolt and nut from raw steel, turned a miniature bat on the lathe, and made a small toolbox for my future tool set. Each day I walked into the shop, I was conscious of the growth I was making with each new project. The results were tangible. I could touch and feel my mistakes. If a spot weld wasn't done right, the two pieces of metal would come apart. It all made sense to me.

My year in metals shop culminated in the creation of a lockbox. I carefully laid out my pattern on the sheet metal and quickly cut it out using the tools and skills I had been developing all year. I bent the metal at the brake, forming the separate box and lid. I welded each corner, carefully fitted the hinge to the lid, and joined it to the box with perfect spot welds. The final step in the assembly was to create the clasp that would allow the box to be locked tight with a small padlock. Upon completion, I carefully filed the sharp edges and applied a coat of rather generic gray paint. The box was perfect. The angles were square, the lid closed exactly, and the clasp lined up perfectly. We took only one test in metals class—the first one. There wasn't a need for a multiple-choice test, fill-in-the-blank quiz, or a single essay. I held my final exam in my hands. The results of my learning were clearly displayed in a rather nondescript, gray, metal box.

RESULTS OF OUR LEARNING

Big data is a big deal these days. Wikipedia defines *big data* as "a broad term for data sets so large or complex that traditional data processing applications are inadequate" (Big data, n.d.). While big data doesn't technically apply to the data we collect as teachers, society's overemphasis on testing can make it feel that way sometimes. Students in grades 3–8 can take between ten and twenty *standardized* tests per year (Lazarín, 2014). And this doesn't include the other assessments—the weekly checks for understanding, the interim tests, the formative tests, the progress-monitoring tests. Students are bombarded with tests. But *we* are bombarded with data. So much data becomes nothing more than noise. It's meaningless.

During my years at Peruvian Park, my teachers and I pored over the test results from the previous year. But how did that help my teachers *specifically*? Sure, we could ability-group students and decide what they needed to relearn, but with such a distance between the identification of student levels of understanding and the self-evaluation of their teaching, how could that help my teachers decide what they needed to change in their instructional practice? And if we teach in the same way this year as we did last year, how does this data help anyone?

My shop teacher wasn't bombarded with data. He used data for growth. He autonomously decided what measures he needed to use in order to determine two things: (1) whether we were learning, and (2) whether he was effectively teaching. His tests weren't high-stakes, but they told him what he needed to know, both about us and about him. Our deliverables were our nondescript metal boxes, but what were his? He probably didn't share his deliverables with anyone. He may not have even documented them. In the early '80s, that wasn't such a big deal—he was still trusted. But in 2015, when society has shifted the focus to an overemphasis on student outcomes as measured by high-stakes tests, we need the proof.

CONNECTED DATA

Data for growth isn't big data. It isn't small data. It's *connected* data. It's data that connects student growth with teacher growth. If the data doesn't connect the two, then it's not meaningful, and somebody isn't growing.

Data for growth helps keep the Big Three in balance. We teach based on our assumptions—our attitudes toward and approaches to teaching. But as we formatively assess our students for understanding, we sometimes find imbalance in the level of growth of different students. This leads us to two actions: to target students (regardless of level) who need intervention and to examine our own teaching strategies.

Let me expand on what I mean with a scenario that I have witnessed countless times in multiple classrooms. It is not uncommon for a student to reach sixth grade without having mastered the basics of long division. This is a skill that is typically introduced in fourth and fifth grades. Once a student reaches sixth grade, it would be easy to assume that he has mastered long division and is ready to take the next step. But what if the student hasn't mastered long division? Consider the following.

Student: (Raises hand)

Teacher: What are you struggling with?

Student: I don't understand how to do this.

Teacher: Oh, you can do this. I know you can.

Student: I just don't get it.

Teacher: OK, let me help you. What is the first thing you need to decide?

Student: I don't know.

Teacher: OK, how many times does seven go into twenty-three?

Student: Four?

Teacher: No, four times seven is twenty-eight. That is too big.

Student: Three?

Teacher: Right! What is seven times three?

Student: Twenty-two?

Teacher: No, it is twenty-one. Put your three right here above this three. Now three times seven is twenty-one so where do we put the twenty-one?

Student: Hmmmmm.

Teacher: You put the twenty-one right below the twenty-three. OK, now we need to subtract twenty-one from twenty-three. OK, now that you have a two right there, we need to ask the question, does seven go into two?

Student: No.

Teacher: OK, so what do we need to do next?

Student: Hmmmmm.

Teacher: Bring down the other three and put it next to the two. Now, can seven go into twenty-three?

Student: Yes.

Teacher: How many times?

Student: Hmmmmm.

Teacher: Remember the last time? Seven went into twenty-three...three times, right?

Student: Right...

The teacher repeats the process of asking questions and helping the student get the right answer, and when he has finished solving the problem she declares, "See, you can do this. Now try the next one, and see if you can do it by yourself. I will come back and check on you in a little bit."

When the teacher goes back to check, she realizes the student still doesn't get it. There's the data: incorrectly completed long division problem. What's the teacher's next step? We don't need to spend too much time analyzing this situation to recognize the problem is not related to long division. The problem is that the teacher didn't make the connection between her student's learning (or lack of it) and her teaching (or lack of it). The data was there—the student showed a lack of understanding during their exchange and completed the next problem incorrectly. It's just that the data wasn't meaningful. The teacher didn't use it to inform her instructional practice. It wasn't data for *growth*. In order for the data to mean something, the teacher needs to evaluate her teaching. How does she approach student questions? Does she dismiss their lack of understanding? (*Oh, you can do this. I know you can.*) How does she handle un-mastered skills, like the student's nonmastery of basic multiplication facts? Does she remediate students? Does she provide cheat sheets? Does she fill in the blanks? How does she approach different students? Does she approach them all in the same way? Does she treat different students differently?

Most teachers, of course, don't teach this way. I also witnessed countless examples of teachers who conscientiously applied in their classrooms the Big Three elements of identifying students' levels of understanding, targeting students for intervention, and self-evaluating their instructional practice. Many of these teachers did this on a consistent basis. But most didn't document it, at least not in much detail. This is where teachers can own the results of the Big Three—through balanced documentation of *all* of the Big Three elements, not just the element of student outcomes.

Society doesn't see us as evaluators, and perhaps we don't either. But we are, and if we aren't, we need to be. If we fail to connect the data in a way that helps both students and us grow, the result is likely to lead to similar and unproductive outcomes. If we fail to document this data for growth, the result is likely to lead to a continued distrust in our ability to teach. But when we begin to focus on how data *specifically* informs our instruction, and when we begin to document that focus, then the Big Three shifts into balance. Then we move toward mastery in our instructional practice. Our student moves toward mastery in his understanding of long division. And our parents move toward trust as they observe both their child's growth and what we did to achieve that growth.

OWNING THE CONVERSATION

Our district had been using standards-based report cards for several years, which gave parents a report of their child's progress in relation to state standards on a four-point scale. To be frank, I had never given much thought to the report cards. I trusted each of my teachers to determine how they would fill out report cards in the best interest of the students.

But one day, a teacher insisted I tell her how to fill out the report card. She wouldn't leave my office until I resolved the matter. I called an ad hoc staff meeting and quickly learned that teachers were interpreting the standards and filling out the report cards in two very different ways. You could have split the faculty right down the middle.

The more traditionally minded teachers were using the standards-based report cards as if they were an updated version of traditional A through F report cards. These teachers sought to train students to do their work and turn assignments in on time, with the hope that student learning would be a byproduct of a schedule of class lectures, assignments, and tests. As a result, these report cards gave parents a snapshot of both test scores and the percentage of work their child had completed.

Other teachers viewed the standards-based report card from a mastery perspective. They subscribed to a mastery-based learning model and believed that while getting work done and turning in assignments were important, student progress should be measured on the principles the child had mastered. They thought of the report cards as a chance to give parents a snapshot of which state standards their child had learned or had not yet learned over the course of the term, not the work their child had completed.

Before I knew it, the battle lines were drawn. The mastery-based teachers held the assumption that students should be assessed on what they knew, not whether or not they had turned in their homework. The traditionally based faculty held the assumption that student behavior was a critical component, not just for assessing students, but also for preparing them for higher education and the workplace.

As we talked, we quickly called to mind bright students who knew their stuff but didn't work particularly hard and other, very conscientious students who turned in everything on time but struggled to master the material. Who was right? Where should the incentives be?

I wasn't able to resolve the divide that day. It took multiple meetings and ongoing conversations. Teachers believed in their approaches. In the end though, after every voice had been heard and the decision had been made to adopt the mastery-based mindset to standards-based reporting, all of the teachers got on board. My teachers and I had engaged in lively conversations that resulted in meaningful accountability. These were conversations based on mutual respect and trust. Conversations that supported autonomy, mastery, and purpose. Conversations we *all* owned about criteria, measures, and reporting.

Conversations like those my faculty and I had about report cards address the accountability we as educators have toward providing consistent criteria, measures, and reporting to our students and their parents. But these types of conversations also provide a safe place for growth: student growth, teacher growth, even administrator growth. As we own the conversations about criteria, measures, and reporting, we establish accountability that makes sense within the larger goals of education. The Big Three elements of identifying student levels of understanding, targeting students for

intervention, and self-evaluating our instructional practice lie at heart of these conversations.

CONVERSATIONS ABOUT CRITERIA

I referred to standards earlier as one of multiple criteria
teachers use to inform and evaluate their implementation of the Big Three. But criteria also encompass
learning outcomes that fall outside that narrow definition of academic standards. Criteria also include
elements that are essential to success in school and in
life but difficult to measure—elements such as motivation, creativity, empathy, artistry, and judgment.
Specific curriculum comes and goes. Trendy instructional practices come and go. Rigorous standards
come and go. But the essential criteria of what we
expect our students to know and do remain essentially unchanged. Teachers understand this, but they
are rarely included in the conversations about criteria.
This is unfortunate on two levels. First, although teachers may not have the extensive background in research
literature that university professors and others in the
educational field have, they have the most *real-life*
experience of anyone. When we leave teachers out of
the conversations about criteria, we are leaving half of

what makes us experts without a voice. The result is that those left creating the latest version of our essentially unchanged criteria are not truly experts. And everyone, even the criteria, suffers for it.

The second unfortunate reason is also fueled by the fact that teachers understand the unchanging nature of criteria. With this understanding in place, they are then being pushed to adopt and implement new methods, new materials, new standards, new tests, and new requirements on a regular basis. I set a timer for five minutes and challenged myself to come up with a random list of new methods and requirements I was expected to implement as a teacher or an administrator:

- Professional learning communities
- Direct instruction
- Response to intervention
- Outcome-based learning
- Standards-based learning
- New math
- Phonics
- Whole language
- Balanced literacy
- Brain research

- Project-based learning
- Portfolios
- Walk-through evaluations
- DIBELS
- AIMSweb
- Discovery learning
- Novels
- Evidence-based learning
- Mastery learning
- Blended learning
- Flipped classrooms
- Multiple textbook adoptions
- Peer evaluation
- Running records
- Magnet schools
- Differentiated instruction
- Action research
- Research-based learning
- Open classrooms
- Multi-age classrooms
- Student directed learning
- Looping
- Music-enhanced learning
- Six traits
- Dual immersion
- Inclusion
- Laser discs with bar coding
- Ability grouping
- Pull-out gifted programs

You may have noticed that many of the different items on my list are very similar or identical to each other in practice. Things that had fallen out of favor in years past are reintroduced with a new name by a new guru. It is interesting to note that I experienced a new strategy on average more than two times per *year.* This list highlights the propensity for change in our schools. It takes time to learn new approaches and time to implement them. And the time teachers spend implementing the latest criterion fad is time lost in improving their instructional practice in truly meaningful ways. But more important, it's trust lost, and respect lost, and *expertise* lost, simply because teachers aren't included in the conversations about criteria.

CONVERSATIONS ABOUT MEASURES

I've discussed many aspects of measures in the section "Balance of Measures," but I want to briefly return to the subject here because we need conversations about who should be collecting measures, and how many there should be.

In the time since *A Nation at Risk*, we've come to accept the idea of external, high-stakes testing as the gold standard for measuring student achievement. Society has not only embraced this approach but has even become a bit blinded to its presence. This is illustrated by Congress's 2015 reauthorization of No Child Left Behind. Although the Every Student Succeeds Act (ESSA) removes current overbearing federal requirements and prohibits federal incursions into state-level accountability, it retains the requirement for annual testing using state-level or nationally-recognized standardized tests for the majority of states, and it requires that states include the results from these tests in their accountability systems (United States of America 114th Congress, 2015).

The problem with *high-stakes* testing is that it tends to distort people's judgment. The problem with *external* testing is that it places accountability in the hands of people who are unfamiliar with the effects that complex human events have on children's learning. The problem with *standardized* testing is that it tends to exacerbate the achievement gap (Madaus & Clarke, 2001). The problem with only using *one test* is that it cannot capture the whole learning of any child. There are a lot of problems with our current approach to accountability. Research doesn't support it (Linn,

2000). Practice doesn't support it. Increasingly, parents around the country don't support it. And so proponents of high-states testing argue that these tests provide an outstanding measure of student levels of understanding (Walberg, 2012). They suggest that teachers can use the data to help provide additional support for students. They argue that the data from these tests help teachers identify areas of strength and weakness in their instructional practice.

But these rationales used by those who advocate this high-stakes, external, standardized, one-test method of accountability are just mimicking what the elements of the Big Three *already* provide.

RATIONALE FOR HIGH-STAKES TESTING	BIG THREE ELEMENTS
Measure student levels of understanding	Identify student levels of understanding
Provide additional support to students	Target students for intervention
Identify areas of strength and weakness in instructional practice	Self-evaluate instructional practice

It's time to test our assumption about what we consider to be the gold standard for measuring student achievement. Given that the elements of the Big Three align to the very rationale used to endorse high-stakes testing, I propose that these elements are the key to establishing a better system of accountability. Whenever we assess our students, we should apply this simple litmus test to check the assessment's value:

Will this assessment directly benefit the individual who takes it?

Let's apply this litmus test to an individual student taking his state's high-stakes end-of-level test. In most cases, the student will experience extensive test preparation that includes multiple practice tests prior to taking the final test. This will consume a considerable amount of class time that could have otherwise been used for more meaningful learning opportunities. The student will eventually take the *real* test, which may consume several hours over the course of a few days. The final results of the test may not be available to the student until after the school year is over. Does this assessment provide direct benefit to this student? The answer is *no*. Our current system of accountability is simply wasting precious time and subjecting students to needless assessments that offer them zero direct benefit. It is wrong.

Now let's apply this litmus test to an individual student taking multiple, low-stakes, formative and summative assessments. In most cases, the student will experience frequent, small, formative quick checks for understanding that help his teacher identify his level of understanding, so that she can adjust her teaching in order to meet his needs. This will consume varying amounts of class time, depending on the class's needs, but this time is filled with meaningful learning opportunities. The student may eventually take a summative test, or he may complete a performance task or project or add to his portfolio a deliverable like my nondescript, gray, metal box. The final results of the formative quick checks are immediate and relevant, and the final results of the summative assessment are immediate and tangible. Do these assessments provide direct benefit to this student? The answer is *yes*. This proposed system of accountability—one that is *already* in place—prioritizes precious time and provides students with opportunities that offer them enormous benefit. It is right.

Teachers are the best equipped to monitor complex human events that affect student learning. They are the best equipped to provide multiple measures of student learning throughout the year. They are the best equipped to provide alternate forms of measures that encourage students of any race or socioeconomic status to thrive. Teachers are the *experts* at testing. Society has been trying to strip this expertise away for decades, but it will never be able to fully strip it away, because society doesn't enter the classroom every day and constantly work to identify student levels of understanding. Politicians and policymakers don't have the *right* to lay claim to accountability around student learning. This should be left up to our communities, educators, parents, and students. And this leads me to my third and culminating conversation: the conversations about reporting.

CONVERSATIONS ABOUT REPORTING

"Our public schools are failing." This refrain is usually supported with evidence gathered from standardized test results. For example, my home state of Utah adopted a letter grade system, using the end-of-level test results, for all of its public K–12 schools. A series of recent articles posted on the website of a local media station highlighted the top and bottom twenty elementary, middle, and high schools based on their scores (Deseret News, 2015). It's tantalizingly tempting to draw unwarranted conclusions from the school rankings, and many outside of education will do just that. But the results are unsurprisingly closely aligned to the socioeconomic makeup of each school's community. This is a fact that will be lost on many who are looking for simple answers to complex problems. It also highlights one of the single biggest reasons we struggle to regain the public's trust: we don't own the conversation about reporting.

We used to own the conversation about reporting. There used to be a local system of accountability that provided checks and balances, not so unlike our federal system of checks and balances. The following graphic illustrates the conversations we owned under this system.

Teachers were accountable to the community (specifically to students and their parents) and to principals. Principals were accountable to the district and to the community. The district was accountable to the community as far as teaching and learning was concerned and to state and federal government in its distribution of government funding. Educators owned the conversations in each of these areas of accountability. Where this original accountability broke down—where teachers lost control of the classroom—was with one assumption that accompanied this original system of accountability. In this original system, teachers were accountable for their *teaching*, not for student *learning*. Students

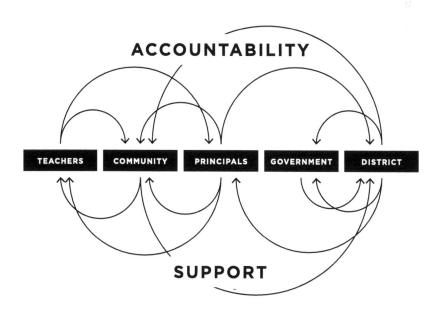

were accountable for that. Because of this assumption, parents blamed any lack of learning on their children, trusting that teacher instruction was adequate.

When *A Nation at Risk* overthrew the assumption of trust in teachers, then the accountability system could no longer sustain itself. Teachers were unprepared to show accountability based on *distrust*. And with a nod of approval from *A Nation at Risk's* fifth recommendation, politicians and others outside of education jumped at the opportunity to take control of the conversations about reporting, without fully understanding the complex nature of teaching and learning. This shift has produced accountability based on simplistic measures that bucket students and schools into grades on a report card that are as likely or more likely to reflect a student's or a school's socioeconomic status as to reflect meaningful student learning.

But the original accountability system is still valid. Good teachers have *always* embraced the understanding that they are accountable for student learning that results from their teaching. Good principals have *always* embraced their role as instructional leaders of their schools. Good districts have *always* supported their schools using finances, time, and resources in ways they can defend to the state and explain to their communities. What's missing is our ownership of the conversations about these existing behaviors.

It's time to return to this new and improved original system of local accountability. I call it new and improved because we are now equipped to own these conversations in the light of trust *or* distrust. We have a deeper understanding of the relationship between teaching and learning as exemplified by the Big Three. We have a better ability to document this relationship through modern technologies. Let's take a brief look at how we can own these conversations today. (For an applied example of these conversations, see Appendix B.)

CONVERSATIONS BETWEEN TEACHERS AND STUDENTS/PARENTS

Teachers can now document, in real time, the progress students are making in their learning. Parents can access this documentation online. The annual parent-teacher conferences and quarterly report cards still exist, but the conversations are no longer limited to these formal snapshots of student learning. They are much more meaningful and relevant in light of this new understanding and better documentation of the Big Three. A single score, whether from a standardized test or as the result of a lengthy student growth process, does not give meaningful or relevant information to the students who take these tests or go through these processes. But when teachers and parents own the conversation about student reporting, parents understand more fully not only what and how their child is learning, but also how their child's teacher is teaching.

CONVERSATIONS BETWEEN TEACHERS AND PRINCIPALS

I've conducted quite a few evaluations over the years. Unlike typical corporate evaluations, which tend to have between five and ten components (Insperity, 2015), teacher evaluations can sometimes have fifty or more elements a teacher must address (Danielson Group, n.d.). This structure can be overwhelming and can sometimes lead to evaluations that are filled with silent observations of nervous teachers and students, predesigned lessons created especially for the evaluation, hit-and-miss artifacts of instructional effectiveness, and most recently, some type of representation of student outcomes. But principals, like teachers, can now document in real time the progress teachers are making in their teaching. Teachers can provide this documentation online. The formal teacher-principal evaluation meetings still exist, but the conversations are no longer limited to these meetings. They can now center on student learning and teacher instruction as it happens in real time. A random walk-through of a classroom, a single representation of student outcomes, a meeting that bundles it all nicely into a thirty-minute package does not give meaningful or relevant information to the teachers who participate in these evaluations. But when teachers and principals own the conversation about teacher instruction, teachers understand more fully how effective their instructional strategies are, and principals can support more fully teachers' efforts to improve them.

CONVERSATIONS BETWEEN PRINCIPALS AND DISTRICTS

I illustrated earlier that many districts have made an about-face, representing state and federal mandates to schools and teachers rather than advocating for their needs to the state and federal government. The federal government drove this about-face by tying federal funding to student outcomes created by the simplistic measures described earlier. And principals had little recourse (or resources) to counter these outside measures with internal documentation of their schools' effectiveness. But districts can now document in real time the progress schools are making in their whole-school improvement of student outcomes. Principals can provide this documentation online. The tug of federal and state mandates still exists, but conversations are no longer limited to the narrow student outcomes required by these mandates. Principals can now provide rich, meaningful documentation of their teachers' and students' progress as it happens in real time. A single grade on a school report card posted in a newspaper online does not give meaningful or relevant information to the principals charged with ensuring effective teacher instruction and meaningful student learning. But when principals and districts own the conversation about school improvement, districts understand more fully the varied and complex needs of their principals' schools and communities, and principals can provide more meaningful data for districts to use in their accountability to communities and the government.

DISTRICT CONVERSATIONS ABOUT ACCOUNTABILITY

As teachers and principals begin to own the conversations about reporting, they empower districts with real-time and relevant data. Districts can then better defend to state and federal government, and better explain to communities, their allocation of finances, time, and resources. They can better defend alternatives to the testing and growth measures that make up our current high-stakes, external accountability system. With this documentation in place, districts will be able to turn back around and fully support their schools and teachers and students in ways that will strengthen and sustain this new and improved original system of local accountability.

This has been a rather ideal description of what needs to happen in order for us to own the conversations about criteria, measures, and reporting. But it is not an unattainable description. Laying claim to accountability is within our reach. But in order for these solutions to take root, we must acknowledge and address two issues.

The first I've described in great detail throughout this book—the need for trust. But not from society. Not yet. Teachers have always had the ability to monitor the "series of complex human events" that contribute to meaningful student learning outcomes. But they cannot do this within the narrow confines of academic standards that are measured by external tests. In order to own their conversations about reporting, they need to be able to incorporate the broader criteria briefly described earlier, and they need to be able to assess students using broader measures than those considered valid and reliable under our current system. And in order to be able to do these things, they need trust, not from society, but from principals and districts. The phrase used by Lincoln is just as applicable here: "A house divided against itself cannot stand." In order to regain the trust of our communities, we must first trust each other.

The second issue we need to address is the issue of noise. Currently, there is a lot of noise around high-stakes accountability and standardized testing and very little noise around continuous learning based on the Big Three elements of identifying student levels of understanding, targeting students for intervention, and self-evaluating instructional practice. If we're to successfully defend a new and improved original system of local accountability, then we need to celebrate the iterative, "do it again" process inherent in continuous learning, and we need to make the conversations we own about what we're doing *noisy*.

OWNING THE NOISE

Walking through the doors of Peruvian Park Elementary for the first time marked the beginning of my career as an elementary school principal. I had been appointed just a week or two before the school year was set to begin, and I was full of self-doubt. I was hoping that no one in the school would know me, thereby helping to conceal the fraud I had perpetuated on those who had given me this opportunity. Entering the office, I was greeted by an incredibly nice woman who introduced herself as Jolene, the head secretary. I quickly introduced myself; peeked into my tiny, walnut-paneled office; and after a bit of nervous conversation, Jolene mentioned that Jackie Sudbury had called earlier that morning.

I had been in the school five minutes, and my cover was already blown. It just so happened that Jackie was a sixth-grade teacher in the building. I didn't know Jackie personally, but I was aware that there was a very strong likelihood she had at one time or another changed my diapers. We both came from relatively large families and grew up in the same small, blue-collar town just two streets apart. When I fell out of a tree and broke my arm, my mom drove me over to Jackie's parents' house to have her mom, who was a nurse, take a look at the damage. Her youngest brother, Ed, and I went to elementary, middle, and high school together. Jackie's husband, John, was my little league football coach. He was a rather big and intimidating guy who pushed his players hard. He was loud, gregarious, and didn't hesitate to make us run laps when we made a mistake. He always managed to balance discipline with praise and had the complete devotion of every kid on the team.

A "DO IT AGAIN" CELEBRATION

"Do it again." The whistle would blow, and the play would be run again. "Do it again. We will stay here all night until we get it right." I can still hear John's booming voice in my head when I think back on those years of little league football. The constant repetition of running plays over and over again until they were perfected was expected. If things didn't go just right, we would huddle up and do it again. Everyone knew the consequences of making a mistake. When John yelled, "Do it again," no one complained—we all just wanted to do our best. We wanted to do it for ourselves, and we wanted to do it for the team.

"Do it again." Mr. Hagen, my sixth-grade teacher was passionate about the arts. He directed the school choir and the school play. I can remember singing the same few lines of one of his favorite songs by the Beatles or practicing the same scene in the school play over and over until we got it just right. "Do it again."

I can hear Coach Sidwell, my junior high basketball coach yelling from the sidelines, "Do it again," and I can hear Coach Kimple, my junior high volleyball coach demanding that we practice setting, bumping, and spiking over and over until we got it right—"Do it again." Mr. Harsh was my junior high drama teacher. He directed our school's master-class performance of *Joseph and the Amazing Technicolor Dream Coat* for which I was cast as Gad. I can still hear him say from the front row of the auditorium, "Do it again."

The greatest benefit of auto shop was getting to work on our own car. I can remember pulling my '72 Beetle into the shop for a quick tune-up. I changed the spark plugs, changed the oil, added new points, and did a static timing. It ran fine when I pulled it in, but when I had completed the tune-up, my car wouldn't start. I called Mac, my auto shop teacher, over and asked for his help. He began by asking a few questions. Did you check the gap on your spark plugs and points? Are you sure you got the timing right? Are the spark plug and coil wires connected? Start at the beginning and check everything again.

One might assume that my days were filled with sports, music, drama, and shop class based on the examples provided. The truth is, the majority of my time was spent in core classes like the rest of my peers. But although these examples come from noncore classes, all teachers, when applying the Big Three elements, apply the same concept of "do it again" determination. What we need now is a "do it again" celebration to go with this determination. Education has focused for so long on preparing for high-stakes tests, that we've coined the term *bubble student* for students who are most likely to test proficient, given extra attention.

We've reduced student learning to a numbers game that focuses on student groups that are most likely to increase our schools' grades, to the detriment of understanding and meeting the individual needs of all students. The iterative Big Three process provides the perfect opportunity for us to continually and visibly showcase each individual student's learning as well as our instructional improvement. It is our opportunity to shift the noise away from meaningless one-shot, high-stakes accountability and the numbers game that accompanies it, and instead celebrate the meaningful instruction and true student learning that happens throughout a school year. The best part about a "do it again" celebration though, is that also provides the perfect opportunity for us to create a noisy grassroots campaign.

THE NOISY GRASSROOTS CAMPAIGN

The pathway to regaining the public trust will invariably be long and complicated. The good news is that we are most likely already doing much of what needs to be done. The bad news is that we're awfully quiet about it.

I conducted a very nonscientific study by searching the following terms: *teachers, teachers in the news, and teachers, news.* The terms produced varying results depending on the search engine. The different searches resulted in more positive or negative portrayals of teachers, depending on the search. But there was one consistency throughout all of the searches: the results tended to be stories *about* teachers or products aimed *at* teachers or strategies *for* teachers. There were very few results *by* teachers.

This book began with the phrase "teaching is an intimate act." Teaching, by its very nature, isn't loud. At its fundamental level, it's about the implementation of the Big Three between one teacher and one student. It's easy for teaching to stay within the confines of the classroom. It's even easier for teaching to stay within the confines of a school. We tend to shut our doors and get down to the business of teaching.

Getting down to the business of teaching is good, except no one sees it. And even those who come in and observe only see part of it, because the Big Three element "self-evaluate instructional practice" is even more intimate than teaching in general. The planning and revising and reflection we do as teachers often never leave the confines of wherever it is we plan, whether at school or at home. To do otherwise is to risk exposure. Exposure of mistakes. Exposure of lack of knowledge. Exposure of ineffective strategies.

The media reinforces our fear of exposure. "Bad" teachers get splashed across the airwaves on a regular basis. (The exact title *bad teachers* even came up first in one of my searches.) This fear of exposure is further fueled by a general societal assumption that teachers should all be experts the moment they step into the classroom. How can we dare to be otherwise?

The solitary nature of teaching and the societal pressure to be instant experts inhibit us from making noise. Sure, we spend our fair share of time sharing ideas on the Internet and through social media, but we seldom venture outside our safe zones. I conducted a second, very nonscientific study by searching "top teacher social media." There were a lot of "how to use this or that social media in your classroom" results, and quite a few "how to effectively use technology in your classroom" results, but again, there were few results devoted to conversations around the Big Three elements that form the foundation of solid instructional practice. And the few I did find tended to be education-specific sites that I would have to sign up for, not public sites that anyone could browse.

When *A Nation at Risk* created a sentiment of distrust around teachers, it created a vacuum of documented accountability that was ultimately filled by the high-stakes, external accountability we have today. Today we have a vacuum of noise around what we're already doing well in our classrooms that is being filled by voices that often vilify public education in general and public education's teachers in particular. It's time to not only own our conversations, but to own our noise.

But how can we do this in face of the fear and natu-ral tendency toward isolation that seems to come with the teaching profession? I'm reminded of a scene in the children's movie *A Bug's Life* (Lasseter & Stanton, 1998) where the grasshoppers are in a bar, joking about how it doesn't matter if an ant stands up to them because the ants are puny. The boss grasshopper plays along for a while, throwing single kernels of grain, which he's using as examples of ants, at the other grasshoppers in jest. But then he breaks the jar holding the grain, and hundreds of kernels smother his unsuspecting underlings. The boss's point was that although one ant working alone couldn't achieve much, all of the ants working together could drive the grasshoppers away.

Some of us are comfortable with speaking out. And to you I say, speak out! Use this strength you have to own our conversations about accountability on the public airways. But for those of us who are a bit more introverted, consider this: there are nearly 3 million K–12 public school teachers educating 55 million students and interacting with approximately 110 million parents in this country. These numbers represent an opportunity to create conversations around our own accountability with close to 35 percent of the *total* population of the United States—noisy conversations that highlight the work we do every day to help meet the individual needs of our students. With every noisy conversation we have with a parent during which we openly and skillfully articulate our understanding and support of her child's needs and abilities and during which we visibly share our efforts and strategies for helping her child learn, we develop trust and gain a voice who can advocate with us and for us.

Don't let yourself be fooled. Our noisy conversations are not a silver bullet we can use to restore balance to the Big Three overnight. It has taken us decades to get to this state of imbalance, after all. But together we can create a noisy grassroots campaign—a campaign of millions of teachers and parents and students all advocating for the return to a new and improved original system of local accountability.

CHAPTER 4

PARTING THOUGHTS

IF WE MEASURE THE SUCCESS OF OUR SCHOOLS BY EXTERNAL, HIGH-STAKES ACCOUNTABILITY, then it would make sense for me to point to my years at Peruvian Park as one of the finest moments of my career. By the metrics deemed valuable under our current system, we were the epitome of what every school tries to achieve. We had high test scores, great teachers, amazing students, and a supportive community. But although I loved working with the teachers and students there, in reality, the most compelling moments of my career were not related to what our current system values. I could point to any number of events that support this assertion, but there are two that stand out in my mind as indicators of true success.

At Heartland, it was a tradition for our PTA to hold an annual end-of-year community carnival: large blow-up slides, climbing walls, and games, the traditional hot-dogs and nachos. On that particular day, I was standing on a hill overlooking the playground and recess fields. The full chaos of students, parents, teachers, and make-shift booths stretched out portentously before me.

While I was taking in the scene, a parent came over to say hello. He was wearing nothing but a pair of tatty denim jeans, and his shirt was tucked into his back pocket exposing his tan and tattooed torso. In another time and place, his presence might have made me uneasy. Not here. I recognized him. He was the father of two of the boys in my school who were regulars in my office.

The youngest boy was a pint-sized kindergartner with long hair to match his father's and a similar proclivity to being bare-chested, which didn't go over so well at school. He was known for picking fights with the older kids. He did this thing where he would stretch his head up to the full four feet of his frame, shake out his locks behind his back, throw out his hands, and threaten anyone who challenged him. Mostly, people didn't.

His older brother was in sixth grade. I'll call him Stan. Stan was big, barrel-chested, and very tall for his age, and it wasn't doing him any favors. He was often seen as an intimidating figure to teachers and the other students, but in truth he was incredibly timid and sensitive. He was easily bullied by his smaller friends and was often the target of older students looking for a fight.

Stan was part of a group of fifth- and sixth-grade boys who were a bit of a motley crew. They all had one thing in common: by 1:00 p.m., their teachers had mostly had enough. I had taken a lot of heat for Stan. There had been incidents and events, voices calling for his suspension. Many of his teachers had grown tired of his angry outbursts and disrespectful retorts. But I felt responsible to him and to his brother, and to their mother whom I consulted with frequently. I felt like we were the last line of defense for Stan. I felt like we had an obligation to do right by him as well as by all the other students in my school just like him. We could. And we had to.

On that afternoon at the carnival, standing with the boys' father, something significant happened. I don't remember what I was wearing, and I doubt his dad recalls either, but I must have looked just as strange to him as he did to me. We were from different tribes. I was struck by how much it didn't matter. He looked at me with the sincerity of a dad who loved his boys and said, "I want to thank you for all you are doing for my boys, especially my oldest." He acknowledged that he hadn't been there for them and regretted his absence, but he wanted me to know that he was grateful. That was it. It was a moment of recognition. Two people whose window of influence over a young man, frankly, had pretty much run its course at that point recognizing for a moment the inherent worth of a boy who deserved better. That moment captured the essence of what we all feel as educators when we are given the opportunity to reflect on the little things, the things that can't be tested.

When I worked as an assistant principal at West Hills Middle School, my principal was a phenomenal woman named Kerrie Naylor. It was a good school with great kids and fantastic teachers. Like every school, we had our fair share of challenges to deal with every day.

At a faculty meeting early in the year, the two guidance counselors got up and informed the faculty that two of our students were dealing with extreme difficulties at home. I remember them explaining, "Each one has a parent who is dying. We need to be super sensitive. These are some things you can do to deal with grief in the classroom..." They went through a number of steps teachers and administrators could take to help a child going through that kind of emotional pain.

One of the teachers raised his hand and asked if the counselors had mentioned the kids' names yet. I am certain every teacher in the room was wondering the same thing. They hadn't. The mood in the room was very somber as everyone pondered the difficulty these students must be facing.

Kerrie stopped the meeting cold. Her response was direct, "Does it matter?" I was actually a little stunned at her tone. My initial thought was, "Of course it matters." It may seem like a very small thing to some, but Kerrie's intensity grabbed my attention. She looked around the room, pausing to make sure everyone was listening and asked a few simple questions. "Shouldn't we treat every student in this school with as much care as possible? Shouldn't we be sensitive to their needs no matter what is going on in their lives? Wouldn't we want to treat every student in that way?"

These two examples contrast starkly with our current system of external, high-stakes accountability. They emphasize the importance of building connections with students and families that all expert educators do so well. They understand that the "series of complex human events" cannot be ignored if a student is to become truly successful in school and in life.

By contrast, external, high-stakes accountability in the form of high-stakes tests (or processes that include high-stakes tests) treats all children as "Stacys" and expects all teachers to be experts from the moment they step into the classroom. But this accountability cannot tell the difference between a Stacy and a Stan. This accountability cannot measure if a student is ill or having a bad day or losing a parent.

External, high-stakes accountability also cannot tell the difference between an expert and a novice teacher. It cannot truly discern between a Peruvian Park and a Heartland. It cannot measure the complexity around student learning or the complexity around teacher instruction. It cannot measure the human connection that is so fundamental to learning and to life. This is not something that external, high-stakes accountability *fails* to do. It is something that it simply *cannot* do.

And yet, we focus so much of our effort, our attention, our energy, on ensuring that students will show growth on the test. We shortchange our students' learning as well as our own growth because we focus on our fear. Fear of test scores that will negatively influence our evaluations and threaten our jobs. Fear of doing *anything* that may detract from student growth as defined by the federal government, even though our discarded actions would most likely be more sensitive to the needs of our students and more effective in ensuring meaningful growth.

But it doesn't have to be this way. Accountability is not the enemy. It's who owns it that matters. External accountability cannot provide a balanced picture of student success; it cannot measure the quality or complexity of instructional practice, and so it focuses instead on the only element of the Big Three it can measure—student learning—and even here, it falls short.

But *we* can provide a balanced approach to the Big Three. We can own our continuous implementation of its three elements. We can own our conversations around criteria, measures, and reporting. We can own our noise. We have more power than we know, but if we are to truly reclaim the classroom, we must willingly own our accountability.

Einstein is quoted as saying, "It's not that I'm so smart, it's just that I stay with problems longer." Taking the path of owning our accountability may not be easy, and it won't be quick, but in the long run, it will be worth it. We have done this before, and we can do this again.

So go ahead, teachers, take the first step. Tell the world what you need to own, and then show the world you can own it. After all is said and done, it is you who will reclaim the classroom.

A LETTER TO THOSE OF YOU WITH FINGERS IN THE EDUCATION PIE

MONEY TALKS. We all know this—it's the elephant in education's room. So for those of us with a finger or two in the education pie, here is some final advice. Feel free to take it or leave it. It's up to you.

TO POLITICIANS AND PHILANTHROPISTS

Maybe you find the information in this book to be a good idea. Maybe it makes sense for teachers to reclaim their classrooms in this way. If it does, then maybe your trigger response is to create a top-down external one-size-fits-all law or program or something (or throw money at a top-down external one-size-fits-all law or program or something) that can homogenize the process and provide that "valid and reliable" accountability you're so used to. Steady there. Take a step back and consider this: We have spent the last thirty-plus years trying the same things over and over and over again with few positive results as defined by the test and many negative results as defined by the impact on real people—on real educators and real families and real children. Our founding fathers had strong feelings about education and the role it needed to play in our society, so there must have been a reason they didn't include it in the Constitution or the Bill of Rights. Local control is necessary in order to meet the needs of local children. A child in the Hamptons has opportunities and levels of support a child in Hamtramck can't even dream of. Each child needs teachers and principals who can meet his individual needs. But local control isn't local if accountability is not. And as soon as a social process—any social process—becomes high stakes, it can no longer accurately measure what it was originally intended to measure. And when you step back and think about it objectively, doesn't it seem a little, well, strange that an entity thousands of miles away with no boots-on-the-ground intel is determining who stays and who goes based, not on their own performance, but on the performance of someone else? So consider that perhaps the road we've been on for thirty years isn't the only road we can take, and keep local in mind when throwing your weight around.

TO TECHNOLOGY AND CONTENT PROVIDERS

You build amazing stuff. The products available to teachers and students are varied and plentiful; they truly have the potential to affect students' lives in positive ways. Many of you are educator-turned-entrepreneur. You have a deep passion for what you're providing and for your ability to help teachers and students in their journey of student learning. I understand. I'm that, too. I am an educator-turned-entrepreneur-sort-of-on-accident who shares the same passion for education. That being said, our products are *tools*, and tools are useless unless someone *uses* them. There are those among us who would like to think that teachers don't have that much of an impact on student learning, that students are weighed down by having to sit in a classroom with peers who may be learning at a faster or slower pace than they are. I'll be the first to agree with you that there are better ways to organize education than the factory-style organization schools currently employ. But there's no better way than a teacher. Students are people. And people need people. It is not enough to give a tool to a student and expect her to learn. She must learn how to learn, and how to *want* to learn, as we all have. Teachers are essential to that step. They provide context and scaffolding and support and mentorship. They model autonomy and mastery and purpose and all the things children need to really succeed in this crazy-paced world. And if they don't, they should. So while you're out there helping to change the world, keep in mind who will have the most impact with the tools you create.

TO THE UNIONS

It's been said that education got the unions it deserved. That's true. In the nineteenth and twentieth centuries, administrators were harsh and arbitrary to educators; they fired them for fickle reasons, made them work in stressful environments, and paid them precious little. Your rise to power helped to counter these injustices. And you were needed. You are still needed. Teachers need you to help empower them—but not with a twenti-eth-century mindset. Teachers need you to look toward them, just as they need administrators to look toward them. They need you to change your public image and, by default, help change theirs. They need you to advocate for their accountability. You have power. But lines have been drawn in the sand between you and others with power. You can choose to stand your ground and face a win-lose scenario. Or you can choose to ignore the battle and advocate for twenty-first-century needs. The choice is yours, but we encourage you to let go of the past and help teachers reclaim their classrooms.

TO PRINCIPALS AND DISTRICT ADMINISTRATORS

Some of you may be excited about this idea of teachers owning their accountability. Some of you may feel a little threatened about the idea. But *all* of you, in your quiet moments, know that the key to any successful implementation of any program or product or plan is not you. It's not your staff. It's not your board. It's not even your students. Your *teachers* can break the best-laid plans and processes—and they can make the most of the worst-laid ones. It may be tempting, especially for those of you who are afraid, to commandeer this idea of a balanced Big Three for punitive evaluative purposes. You may not even realize you're doing it. You may be mentally fitting these ideas into a current, prescriptive evaluation process even as you read this. If this is the case: breathe. Take a step back. Remember a time when teachers were trusted—and trust them. Build an evaluation process that empowers teachers. Build an evaluation process that supports teachers. Build a process that teachers *want* to be a part of, that they don't feel they need a "special lesson" for. A process built on mutual respect and an understanding that it is the *journey* that matters, not the destination. The moment these ideas become punitive, they lose their effectiveness. Remember, mastery learning applies to everyone, not just students, and it relies on respect for others.

TO TEACHERS

This entire book is for you, so why are you included here? Because you have a finger in the education pie—a lot of fingers in the pie, actually. You may not have money to throw around. You may not *think* you have power either, but if you think that way, you're mistaken. You have more power than you know. Anything you support can succeed, and everything you don't will fail. That's power. Our society has led you to believe that you are not good enough. But you are good enough. As I said before, taking the path of owning your accountability won't be easy, and it won't be quick, but in the long run, it will be worth it. So go ahead, take the first step. And if you don't think this is the way to own your accountability, then tell us so. Tell the world what you need own, and then show the world you can own it. After all is said and done, it is you who will reclaim your classroom.

OWNING THE CONVERSATION: REPORTING EXAMPLES

BELOW ARE APPLIED EXAMPLES USING MASTERYCONNECT, as the supporting technology platform. These examples illustrate three of the conversations discussed in Chapter Three: Conversations between teachers and students/parents, conversations between teachers and principals, and conversations between principals and districts.

These examples aren't comprehensive, but they do provide a window into the kinds of documentation available to help support you in your efforts to lay claim to accountability as you own the results of the Big Three, own your conversations, and own the noise. Visit masteryconnect.com if you'd like to learn more about how these and other features can help support you in your efforts to reclaim your classrooms.

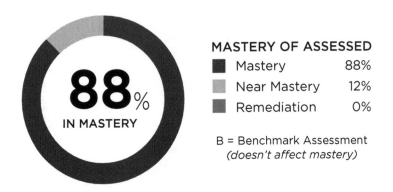

CONVERSATIONS BETWEEN TEACHERS AND STUDENTS/PARENTS

Teachers can document, in real time, the progress students are making in their learning, and parents can access this documentation online. For example, Mckenzie's parents can view her overall progress in third-grade math standards in real time. This is illustrated in two ways: the graphic above shows she's in mastery for eighty-eight percent of the standards, and the bar graph below shows the percentage of standards assessed. They can also see her level of mastery on individual standards and can expand a standard to see details of her progress for that standard.

M	3.OA.A.1	Interpret products of whole numbers, e.g., interpret 5 x 7...	▼
M	3.OA.A.2	Interpret whole-number quotients of whole numbers, e.g...	▼
NM	3.OA.A.3	Interpret multiplication and division within 100 to solve...	▼

Mckenzie's parents can click on individual assessments to see details by assessment, if the teacher has shared them. Her parents can also view notes provided by the teacher and initiate an email directly from the report.

Mckenzie's teacher can reword standards into parent- and student-friendly "I can" statements. He can also include notes about instructional strategies that are helping Mckenzie learn and provide quick tips for the parents on how to help Mckenzie at home.

Mckenzie's information enters the report in real time as she completes assessments, so her parents don't have to wait for a parent-teacher conference or rely on Mckenzie's backpack-organization skills to view her latest progress. They can initiate a conversation with Mckenzie's teacher at any time, and Mckenzie's teacher can do the same.

When teachers and parents own the conversation using a student progress report such as this one, parents understand more fully not only what and how their child is learning, but also how their child's teacher is teaching.

CONVERSATIONS BETWEEN TEACHERS AND PRINCIPALS

Principals, like teachers, can document in real time the progress teachers are making in their teaching, and teachers can provide this documentation online. For example, as Mr. Smith assesses formatively in his classroom, he can see patterns emerging within his mastery tracker. Many of his students are struggling with the concept of positive and negative numbers having opposite directions or values, and Joel seems to be struggling with most of the concepts being taught. Mr. Smith can use this information to inform his own instruction, and he can also leverage the experience of

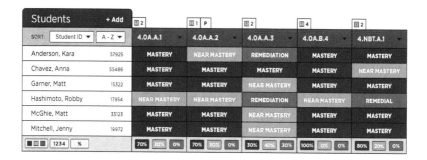

his principal, as the instructional leader of the school, to explore additional strategies and ideas.

Mr. Smith's principal can draw on this real-time information to better support Mr. Smith's specific instructional needs. She can also better meet the needs of individual students within her school by identifying students with similar struggles across classrooms.

When teachers and principals own the conversation about teacher instruction, teachers understand more fully how effective their instructional strategies are, and principals can support more fully teachers' efforts to improve them.

CONVERSATIONS BETWEEN PRINCIPALS AND DISTRICTS

Districts can document in real time the progress schools are making in their whole-school improvement of student outcomes. Principals can provide this documentation online. For example, the district administrators in Washington district can view real-time progress for all

Percentage of Progress for Washington School

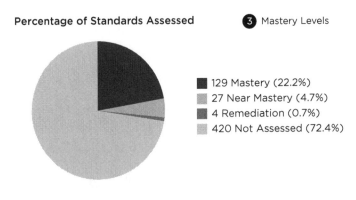

Percentage of Standards Assessed   3 Mastery Levels

- 129 Mastery (22.2%)
- 27 Near Mastery (4.7%)
- 4 Remediation (0.7%)
- 420 Not Assessed (72.4%)

Mastery of Standards Assessed

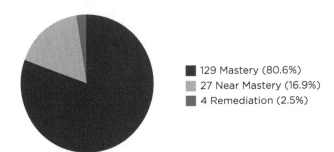

- 129 Mastery (80.6%)
- 27 Near Mastery (16.9%)
- 4 Remediation (2.5%)

of the schools within the district and target support for those schools that may be struggling. School principals can provide additional insight into issues that may be affecting performance, so that the district can meet specific school needs, as they're needed.

District administrators can also view immediate results for districtwide assessments. When administrators see that students seem to be struggling with division of fractions, they can explore two immediate possibilities: students are indeed struggling with division of fractions, or the items aligned to that standard need to

Mastery for Hewitt Academy

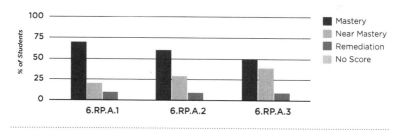

Mastery for Madawaska K-8 School

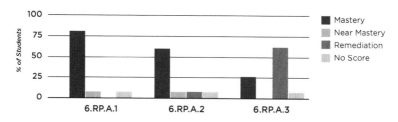

be revised. They can also see that the Madawaska K-8 school seems to be struggling overall and can immediately provide additional support.

When principals and districts own the conversation about school improvement, districts understand more fully the varied and complex needs of their principals' schools and communities, and principals can provide more meaningful data for districts to use in their accountability to communities and the government.

REFERENCES

4President Corporation. (n.d.). George W. Bush for President 2000 Campaign Brochure 'Opportunity, Security and Responsibility–A Fresh Start for America'. Retrieved from http://www.4president.org/brochures/georgewbush2000brochure.htm

Bandura, A. (1977). Self-efficacy: Toward a unifying theory of behavioral change. *Psychological Review, 84*(2).

Bay, M. (Director). (1998). *Armageddon* [Motion picture]. United States: Buena Vista Pictures.

BBC News. (2014). Barrowford school's KS2 'proud' letter to pupils goes viral. Retrieved from http://www.bbc.com/news/uk-england-lancashire-28319907

Big data. (n.d.). In *Wikipedia*. Retrieved from https://en.wikipedia.org/wiki/Big_data

Bloom, B. S. (1968). Learning for Mastery. Instruction and Curriculum. Regional Education Laboratory for the Carolinas and Virginia, Topical Papers and Reprints, Number 1. *Evaluation Comment, 1*(2).

Bolduan, K. (2008). "100 mph" school chief seeks "radical changes." CNN. Retrieved from http://www.cnn.com/2008/LIVING/wayoflife/09/09/dc.schools/index.html?eref=rss_us

Brooks-Gunn, J., & Duncan, G. J. (1997). The effects of poverty on children. *Children and Poverty*, 7(2). Retrieved from https://www.princeton.edu/futureofchildren/publications/docs/07_02_03.pdf

Burton, T. (Director). (2005). *Charlie and the Chocolate Factory* [Motion picture.]. United States: Warner Brothers.

Bush, G. (1990). Address before a joint session of the Congress on the State of the Union. Retrieved from http://www.presidency.ucsb.edu/ws/?pid=18095

Campbell, D. T. (1976). *Assessing the impact of planned social change*. Retrieved from http://portals.wi.wur.nl/files/docs/ppme/Assessing_impact_of_planned_social_change.pdf

Carnine, D. (2000). Why education experts resist effective practices (and what it would take to make education more like medicine). Retrieved from http://edexcellence.net/publications/edexpertsresist.html

Chase, S. P. (1862). The Negroes at Port Royal: Report of E. L. Pierce, Government Agent to the Hon. Salmon P. Chase, Secretary of the Treasury. Boston: R. F. Wallcut.

Chingos, M. M., Whitehurst, G. J., & Lindquist, K. M. (2014). *School superintendents: Vital or irrelevant?* Washington, DC: Brown Center on Education Policy.

Cuban, L. (2004). The open classroom. *Education Next, 4*(2). Retrieved from http://educationnext.org/theopenclassroom/

Danielson Group. (n.d.). The framework. Retrieved from https://www.danielsongroup.org/framework/

DeLay, D. (2008). Teaching is a very complex social art form. *Educator*, 39.

Deseret News. (2015). Grading Utah schools, 2015: Top 20 highest scoring elementary schools. Retrieved from http://www.deseretnews.com/top/3399/0/Grading-Utah-schools-2015-Top-20-highest-scoring-elementary-schools.html

Desjardins, R. (2015). The precarious role of education in identity and value formation processes: The shift from state to market forces. *European Journal of Education, 50*(2).

Dewey, J. (1938). *Experience & Education*. New York: Simon & Schuster.

Di Carlo, M. (2011). The evidence on charter schools and test scores. Retrieved from http://www.shankerinstitute.org/sites/shanker/files/blog/2011/12/CharterReview.pdf

Donald DeLay obituary. (2011, December 14). *Vermont Standard*. Retrieved from http://www.thevermontstandard.com/2011/12/donald-delay-84-obituary/

Donner, R. (Director). (1985). *The Goonies* [Motion picture]. United States: Warner Brothers.

Dorn, S. (2010). The political dilemmas of formative assessment. *Exceptional Children, 76*(3).

EconomicsHelp.org. (n.d.). Definition of public good. Retrieved from http://www.economicshelp.org/ micro-economic-essays/marketfailure/public-goods/

Felton, E. (2015). Are new Common Core tests really better than the old multiple-choice tests? *The Hechinger Report*. Retrieved from http://hechingerreport.org/ are-new-common-core-tests-really-better-than-the-old-multiple-choice-tests/

Freedman, D. H. (2010). Lies, damn lies, and medical science. *The Atlantic*. Retrieved from http:// www.theatlantic.com/magazine/archive/2010/11/ lies-damned-lies-and-medical-science/308269/

FreedomWorks. (2011). Top 10 reasons to support school choice Senate Bill 1 in Pennsylvania. Retrieved from http:// www.freedomworks.org/content/top-10-reasons-support-school-choice-senate-bill-1-pennsylvania-0

Ganem, J. (2011, July 7).Test scores vs. accountability. *The Baltimore Sun*. Retrieved from http://articles.baltimoresun. com/2011-07-07/news/bs-ed-test-scores-20110707_1_test-scores-accountability-zero-tolerance-policies

Gardner, D. P. (2005). *Earning my degree: Memoirs of an American university president.* Oakland, CA: University of California Press.

Gill, B., Bruch, J, & Booker, K. (2013). *Using alternative student growth measures for evaluating teacher performance: what the literature says.* (REL 2013–002). Washington, DC: U.S. Department of Education, Institute of Education Sciences, National Center for Education Evaluation and Regional Assistance, Regional Educational Laboratory Mid-Atlantic. Retrieved from http://ies.ed.gov/ncee/edlabs

Glass, I. (2010). NUMMI. *This American Life* [Audio podcast]. Retrieved from http://www.thisamericanlife.org/radio-archives/episode/403/nummi

Goldstein, D. (2014). The teacher wars: A history of America's most embattled profession. New York: Random House.

Head Teacher. (n.d.) In *Wikipedia*. Retrieved from https://en.wikipedia.org/wiki/Head_teacher

Hechinger Report, The. (2014). Number of U.S. charter schools up 7 percent, report shows. Retrieved from http://www.usnews.com/news/articles/2014/11/03/number-of-us-charter-schools-up-7-percent-report-shows

Honeywell, R. J. (1931). *The educational work of Thomas Jefferson.* Cambridge, MA: Harvard University

Press. Retrieved from https://archive.org/details/
educationalworko012284mbp

HuffPost Politics. (2013). How poverty impacts
students' test scores, in 4 graphs. Retrieved from http://
www.huffingtonpost.com/2013/11/19/poverty-test-
scores_n_4298345.html

Insperity. (2015). Completed examples. Retrieved from
https://www.performancereview.com/pfasp/compex.asp

Johnson, J. O., Kominski, R., Smith, K., & Tillman, P.
(2005). *Changes in the Lives of U.S. Children: 1990–2000.*
Retrieved from https://www.census.gov/population/www/
documentation/twps0078/twps0078.pdf

Johnson, L. B. (1965). Special message to the Congress:
Toward Full Educational Opportunity. Retrieved from
http://www.presidency.ucsb.edu/ws/?pid=27448

Jones, G. M., Jones, B. D., Hardin, B., Chapman, L.,
Yarbrough, T., & Davis, M. (1999). The impact of high-stakes
testing on teachers and students in North Carolina. *Phi
Delta Kappan*, 201.

Jones, R. P., Cox, D., Navarro-Rivera, J., Dionne, Jr., E. J.,
& Galston, W. A. (2013). Do Americans believe capitalism
and government are working? Retrieved from http://www.
brookings.edu/research/reports/2013/07/18-economic-
values-survey-capitalism-government-prri-dionne-galston

Lacour, M., & Tissington, L. D. (2011). The effects of poverty on academic achievement. *Educational Research and Reviews*, 6(7), 522–527.

Ladd, H. F. (2002). *Market-based reforms in urban education*. Washington, DC: Economic Policy Institute.

Lasseter, J., & Stanton, A. (Directors). (1998). *A bug's life* [Motion picture]. United States: Walt Disney Pictures.

Lazarín, M. (2014). *Testing overload in America's schools*. Retrieved from https://cdn.americanprogress.org/wp-content/uploads/2014/10/LazarinOvertestingReport.pdf

Leung, R. (Correspondent). (2004, January 4). The 'Texas Miracle.' *60 Minutes*. CBS Television Network.

Lewis, B. (n.d.). Pros and cons of merit pay for teachers: Should teachers be rewarded for performance like everyone else? Retrieved from http://k6educators.about.com/od/assessmentandtesting/a/meritypay.htm

Linn, R. L. (2000). Assessments and accountability. *Educational Researcher*, 29(2).

Madaus, G.F., & Clarke, M. (2001). *The Adverse Impact of High Stakes Testing on Minority Students: Evidence from 100 Years of Test Data*. Retrieved from http://files.eric.ed.gov/fulltext/ED450183.pdf

Market Economy. (n.d.). In *Dictionary.com*. Retrieved from http://dictionary.reference.com/browse/market-economy?s=t

Morrison, N. (2013). Merit pay for teachers is only fair. Retrieved from http://www.forbes.com/sites/nickmorrison/2013/11/26/merit-pay-for-teachers-is-only-fair/

National Center for Education Statistics. (2000). *Dropout rates in the United States: 1999*. Retrieved from http://nces.ed.gov/pubs2001/2001022.pdf

National Center for Education Statistics. (2001). *Outcomes of learning: Results from the 2000 Program for International Student Assessment of 15-Year-Olds in Reading, Mathematics, and Science Literacy*. Retrieved from http://nces.ed.gov/pubs2002/2002115.pdf

National Center for Education Statistics. (2003). *Overview and inventory of state education reforms: 1990 to 2000*. Retrieved from https://nces.ed.gov/pubs2003/2003020.pdf

National Center for Education Statistics. (2005). *Violence in U.S. public schools: 2000 school survey on crime and safety*. Retrieved from http://nces.ed.gov/pubs2004/2004314.pdf

National Center for Education Statistics. (n.d.a). *National Assessment of Adult Literacy (NAAL)*. Retrieved from https://nces.ed.gov/naal/kf_demographics.asp

National Center for Education Statistics. (n.d.b). *National Assessment of Educational Progress (NAEP): Frequently asked questions*. Retrieved from https://nces.ed.gov/nationsreportcard/faq.aspx

National Commission on Excellence in Education. (1983). *A nation at risk: The imperative for educational reform*. Retrieved from http://www2.ed.gov/pubs/NatAtRisk/risk.html

National Governors Association Center for Best Practices and Council of Chief State School Officers. (n.d.). Key shifts in mathematics. Retrieved from http://www.corestandards.org/other-resources/key-shifts-in-mathematics/

National School Boards Association. (n.d.). Elementary and Secondary Education Act Reauthorization (ESEA). Retrieved from https://www.nsba.org/advocacy/federal-legislative-priorities/elementary-and-secondary-education-act-reauthorization-esea

New York State Archives. (n.d.). Federal education policy and the states, 1945–2009: The George H. W. Bush years: Education summit. Retrieved from http://www.archives.nysed.gov/edpolicy/research/res_essay_bush_ghw_edsummit.shtml

Nichols, S. L., & Berliner, D. C. (2005). The inevitable corruption of indicators and educators through high-stakes testing. Retrieved from http://epsl.asu.edu/epru/documents/EPSL-0503-101-EPRU.pdf

Niles, H. (Ed.). (1822–1823). Public education interesting letters. *Niles' Weekly Register, 23*, 377.

North Texas Regional Consortium. (2012). Letter to members of the Texas legislature. Retrieved from https://tcta.org/sites/tcta.org/files/northtexasregionalconsortium_0.pdf

Ohno, T. (1988). *Toyota production system: Beyond large-scale production.* Portland, OR: Productivity Press.

Owens, A., & Mims, B. (2014). Hundreds of teachers leaving Wake Schools; pay cited. Retrieved from http://www.wral.com/-alarming-wake-teacher-turnover-numbers-to-be-released-thursday/13576437/

Pew Research Center. (2011). Little change in public's response to "Capitalism," "Socialism": A political rhetoric test. Retrieved from http://www.people-press.org/2011/12/28/little-change-in-publics-response-to-capitalism-socialism/

Pink, D. (2009). The puzzle of motivation [TED Talk]. Retrieved from http://www.ted.com/talks/dan_pink_on_motivation?language=en

Pink, D. (2011). *Drive: The surprising truth about what motivates us.* New York: Riverhead Books.

Porter, T. M. (n.d.). Theodore M. Porter Distinguished Professor of History. Retrieved from http://www.history.ucla.edu/people/faculty/faculty-1/faculty-1?lid=384

Ravitch, D. (2010). *The death and life of the great American school system: How testing and choice are undermining education*. New York: Basic Books.

Rothman, M. A. (1972). *Discovering the natural laws: The experimental basis of physics*. North Chelmsford, MA: Courier Corporation.

Shanteau, J. (1992). Competence in experts: The role of task characteristics. *Organizational Behavior and Human Decision Processes, 53*(2).

Simons, D. (2010). *The monkey business illusion* [YouTube video]. Retrieved from https://www.youtube.com/watch?v=IGQmdoK_ZfY

Sternberg, R. J. (2009). Wisdom, intelligence, and creativity synthesized: A new model for liberal education. *Liberal Education, 95*(4). Retrieved from https://www.aacu.org/publications-research/periodicals/wisdom-intelligence-and-creativity-synthesized-new-model-liberal

Sternberg, R. J., Bonney, C. R., Gabora, L., & Merrifield, M. (2012). WICS: A model for college and university admissions. *Educational Psychologist, 47*(1), 30–41.

Sternberg, R. J., & the Rainbow Project Collaborators. (2006). The Rainbow Project: Enhancing the SAT through assessments of analytical, practical, and creative skills. Retrieved from http://f20.blog.uni-heidelberg.de/files/2008/02/the-rainbow-project.pdf

Strauss, V. (2014). Kindergarten teacher: My job is now about tests and data – not children. I quit. *Washington Post*. Retrieved from https://www.washingtonpost.com/blogs/answer-sheet/wp/2014/03/23/kindergarten-teacher-my-job-is-now-about-tests-and-data-not-children-i-quit/

Twomey, R. (2008). How to fix America's schools. *TIME, 172*(23), cover.

United States of America 103d Congress. (1993). *Goals 2000: Educate America Act* (H.R. 1804). Retrieved from http://www2.ed.gov/legislation/GOALS2000/TheAct/index.html

United States of America 107th Congress. (2002). Public Law 107–110. Retrieved from http://www2.ed.gov/policy/elsec/leg/esea02/107-110.pdf

United States of America 114th Congress. (2015). *Every Student Succeeds Act* (H.R. Rep. No. 114-354). Retrieved from https://www.gpo.gov/fdsys/pkg/CRPT-114hrpt354/pdf/CRPT-114hrpt354.pdf

U.S. Department of Education. (n.d.). Competency-based learning or personalized learning. Retrieved from http://www.ed.gov/oii-news/competency-based-learning-or-personalized-learning

U.S. Department of Education. (1991). *America 2000: An education strategy: Sourcebook*. Retrieved from http://files.eric.ed.gov/fulltext/ED327985.pdf

U.S. Department of Education. (2009). *Race to the Top Program Executive Summary.* Retrieved from https://www2.ed.gov/programs/racetothetop/executive-summary.pdf

U.S. Department of Education. (2012). *ESEA flexibility.* Retrieved from http://www2.ed.gov/policy/elsec/guid/esea-flexibility/index.html

Walberg, H. J. (2012). Standardized Tests Effectively Measure Student Achievement. In D. Brynfonski (Ed.) *Standardized Testing.* Detroit: Greenhaven Press. Retrieved from http://ic.galegroup.com/ic/ovic/ViewpointsDetailsPage/DocumentToolsPortletWindow?displayGroupName=Viewpoints&jsid=1b334a273f43077aa7f9efe45fc4b0f7&action=2&catId=&documentId=GALE%7CEJ3010478217&u=over80203&zid=73c91ade3bc854f19777ea773e9646f8

Washburne, C. W. (1922). Educational measurement as a key to individual instruction and promotions. *The Journal of Educational Research, 5*(3).

Waters, T., Marzano, R. J., & McNulty, B. (2003). Balanced leadership: What 30 years of research tells us about the effect of leadership on student achievement. A working paper. Retrieved from http://www.mcrel.org/~/media/Files/McREL/Homepage/Products/01_99/prod82_BalancedLeadership.ashx

Weir, P. (Director). (1989). *Dead poets society* [Motion picture]. United States: Touchstone Pictures.

Wiener, G. (2014). Why I quit teaching after 33 years. *The Week*. Retrieved from http://theweek.com/articles/445635/why-quit-teaching-after-33-years

Young, R. (Host). (2013, July 31). Crisis in Philadelphia schools comes to a head. *Here and Now with Robin Young and Jeremy Hobson*. NPR and WBUR Boston.

Continue the discussion at

www.reclaimingtheclassroom.com

Made in the USA
Charleston, SC
23 January 2016